Success in Maths

Rowena Onions
Chris Onions
Jacqueline Pendergast
Garry Pendergast
Series Editor: Jayne de Courcy

BOOK 1
Ages 9–11

Contents

Collins Educational
An Imprint of HarperCollins*Publishers*

The 3 Steps to Success...

Step 1

Key skills practice

- *Success in Maths Book 1* provides practice in a number of important Maths skills. These skills, which are developed further in Books 2–4, are the ones that your child needs to master in order to achieve a high level in the Maths National Test at the end of Key Stage 2.
- Each chapter takes one Maths skill and gives your child practice in it, in straightforward steps using graded questions.
- This in-depth practice ensures that your child will achieve real understanding of each skill.

Step 2

Practice with National Test Questions

- The book contains three sections of *National Test Questions*. These questions have been included to test the skills covered in the chapters.
- Your child can do these Test questions immediately after working on the skills chapters. You might, however, prefer to wait and ask your child to do them a little later to check that the skills have been thoroughly mastered.

Step 3

Improving your child's performance

- The book contains detailed *Answers and Guidance* to both the skills practice questions and the *National Test Questions*.
- The authors, who are KS2 Test Examiners, provide detailed guidance, showing how to go about answering the questions correctly.
- In this way, you can work with your child to improve both skills and performance in the KS2 Maths National Test.

Help with timing

- ★ As the Maths National Test papers are timed, it is important that your child learns to answer questions within a time limit.
- ★ Each skills chapter and each *Test Questions* section gives target times for answering the questions. If you choose to, you can ask your child to time how long it takes to answer the questions. You can then compare your child's time against the target times provided. In this way, you will form a good idea of whether your child is working at the right rate to complete the Maths National Test papers successfully.

Progression

- ★ *Success in Maths* is aimed at 9–11 year-olds who are in Years 5 and 6 of primary school. There is in-built progression: each book builds on skills covered in previous books.
- ★ To get the most out of *Success in Maths*, it is important that your child works through all four books in sequence. If you are buying this series for your child who is aged 9/10 (Year 5), then buy Books 1 and 2, and Books 3 and 4 at age 10/11 (Year 6). If your child is already in Year 6, then it is still advisable to work through from Book 1 to Book 4, to ensure that your child benefits from the progression built into the series.

Note to teachers

- ★ This book, and the other five titles in the *Success in Maths* series, are designed for use at home and in schools in Years 5 and 6. They focus on the key Maths skills that will raise children's performance in the Maths National Test.
- ★ You can use the books in class or give them to children for homework to ensure that they are fully prepared for their Maths National Test.

1 Number patterns

What's it all about?

- In your Maths National Test you may be asked to find the missing numbers in a pattern (or sequence) of numbers.
- Before you can find the missing numbers, you need to work out a 'rule' for the sequence.
- The questions in this chapter show you ways to discover and use adding and subtracting rules to build number patterns.

> To build the simplest number sequences, just add or subtract the same number over and over again.

1 Find the 'rules'. The first one has been done for you.

Sequence:	**Rule:**
a) 2 4 6 8 10	Add two each time.
b) 6 9 12 15 18	Add three each time.
c) 5 14 23 32 41	Add nine each time.
d) 25 21 17 13 9	Subtract four each time.
e) 31 24 17 10 3	Subtract seven each time.

2 Finish these sequences.

a) 1 7 13 19 25 31

b) 24 20 16 12 8 4

c) 15 27 39 51 63 75

d) 33 28 23 18 13 8

e) 1 12 23 34 45 66

f) 100 82 64 36 8 -20

In some sequences the rule is not so simple. First work out the 'gap' between one number and the next in the sequence by adding or subtracting. For example:

1 add 2 3 add 3 6 add 4 10

> In these sequences, you always need to add or subtract. In more difficult sequences you may need to use multiplication and division. This is covered in Book 2.

3 Use addition or subtraction to work out the gaps for each of these sequences. The first one has been done for you.

a) 19 subtract 2 17 subtract 3 14 subtract 4 10

b) 15 4 19 2 21 4 25

c) 29 Subract 12 17 Subract 6 11 Subroct 3 8

d) 34 11 45 11 56 11 67

e) 27 15 42 13 55 11 66

4 The gaps between the numbers follow a rule.
Find the rules. The first two have been done for you.

a) 1 ___add 2___ 3 ___add 3___ 6 ___add 4___ 10

Rule: The gap between the numbers increases by one each time.

b) 27 ___subtract 4___ 23 ___subtract 3___ 20 ___subtract 2___ 18

Rule: The gap between the numbers decreases by one each time.

c) 6 8 12 18 26
Gap: ______ ______ ______ ______
Rule: ____________________

d) 6 5 8 7 10
Gap: ______ ______ ______ ______
Rule: ____________________

e) 29 24 32 27 35
Gap: ______ ______ ______ ______
Rule: ____________________

A rule for a sequence describes the pattern you can find from the information you are given.

5 Find the rule.

a) 8 14 21 29 38 48 **Rule:** ____________
b) 28 30 27 29 26 28 **Rule:** ____________
c) 1 6 11 14 17 22 27 **Rule:** ____________
d) 1 3 6 5 7 10 9 **Rule:** ____________

Sometimes more than one rule will work for the same sequence of numbers.

6 Complete these number sequences.

a) 44 36 28 ___ ___ ___
b) 2 13 24 ___ ___ ___
c) 17 19 24 26 31 ___ 38 40 ___ ___
d) 20 ___ 28 32 ___ ___ 44
e) 14 ___ 28 35 ___ ___ 56

Test question

Write in the missing numbers in this number sequence.

4 7 9 12 14 ___ 19 22 ___

Answers and Guidance are given on p.36.

How long did you take?

2 Using timetables

What's it all about?

- ★ You need to be able to understand and use information given in timetables.
- ★ To understand a timetable, you must be able to read the 24-hour clock.
- ★ To answer some types of question about timetables, you need to be able to add and subtract hours and minutes.

Here is a train timetable:

Station	Arrival time
Worthing	07.24
Lancing	07.28
Shoreham	07.33
Portslade	07.38
Hove	07.41
Haywards Heath	07.59
Gatwick Airport	08.11
East Croydon	08.28
Clapham Junction	08.39
London Victoria	08.47

1 a) What time does the train arrive at Hove? 07.41

b) How long does it take to travel between:

i) Worthing and Lancing 4 minites

ii) Lancing and Shoreham 5 minites

iii) Haywards Heath and Gatwick 12 mintes

iv) Hove and East Croydon 36 minites

v) Worthing and London Victoria? 1 hour 23 mins

c) What is the shortest journey time between stations?

3 minites

d) What is the longest journey time between stations?

1 hour 23 mins

Sometimes you need to 'read between the lines', i.e. to work out information that is not given, from the information that is given.

2 a) Does the train arrive at Gatwick in time to meet an 08.00 flight?

NO

b) Between which two stations is the train, if the time is 07.50?

Hove and Haywards health

c) Between which two stations is the train, if the time is 08.25?

Gatwick airport & East croydon

d) If the train is 5 minutes late, what time will it arrive at Haywards Heath? 08.04

e) If there is a delay at Gatwick Airport and the train doesn't leave until 08.27, but then it travels at its normal speed, what time will it arrive in London? ______

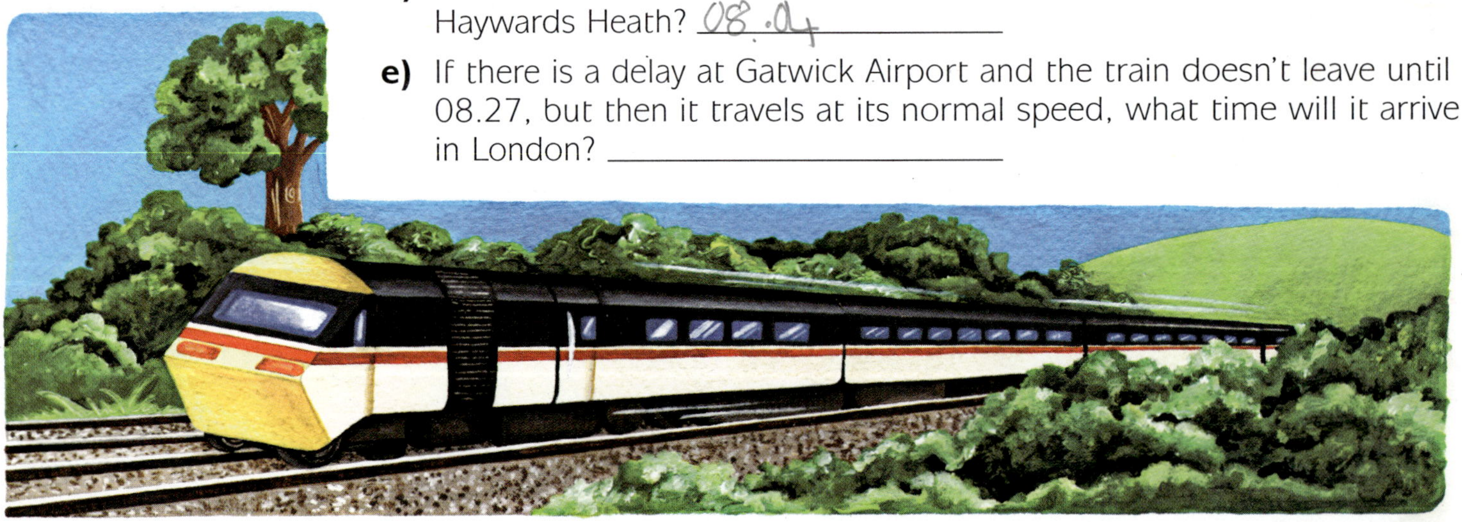

3 The 20A bus and the 49 bus both start and finish their journeys at the same places, but they follow different routes. Here are their timetables.

Bus 20A			Bus 49		
Arrives		Departs	Arrives		Departs
07.00	Eastham	07.02	07.00	Eastham	07.03
07.30	Eastburn	07.32	07.30	Northern	07.33
08.00	Northern	08.02	08.00	Westable	08.04
08.30	Northbourne	08.32	08.30	Eastable	08.32
09.00	Northable	09.02	09.00	Southam	09.02
09.30	Southam	09.32	09.30	Westburn	09.32
10.00	Southourne		10.00	Southourne	

a) Which bus arrives at Southam first? ______

b) How long does it take for the 20A to get from Eastham to Southam? ______

c) Which bus goes to Westable? ______

d) If the 20A is leaving Northbourne at 08.32 where is the 49?

______

Test question

Here are the times of some television programmes.

CHANNEL 1	
7.00	CARTOON
7.15	FILM
9.00	NEWS
9.30	WEATHER
9.35	SPORT
10.20	DRAMA

CHANNEL 2	
7.00	LOCAL NEWS
7.45	QUIZ SHOW
8.30	COMEDY
9.00	HOSPITAL DRAMA
10.00	POP CHART
10.40	FILM

1 What is showing on Channel 2 at ten minutes to eight?

______

2 Tom watches Hospital Drama and then changes to Channel 1 at the end. What is showing on Channel 1 when he changes channel?

______

3 The film on Channel 2 starts at 10.40. It lasts for one and a half hours. At what time does the film end?

______

Answers and Guidance are given on pp.36-37.

How long did you take?

3 Drawing 2D shapes

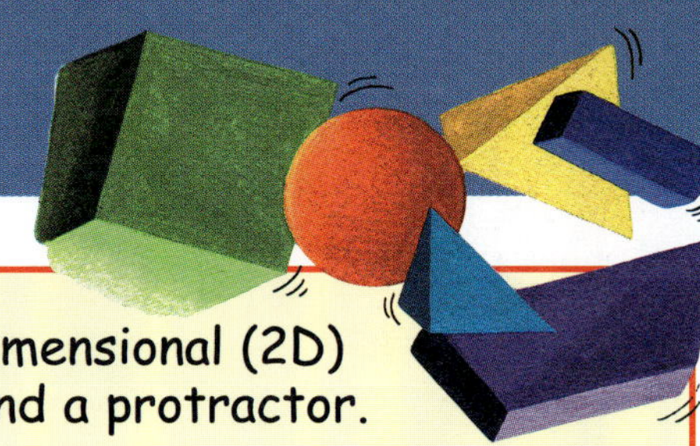

What's it all about?

- This chapter will remind you how to draw two-dimensional (2D) squares and triangles accurately, using a ruler and a protractor.
- To draw these shapes you need to understand about their properties, i.e. the rules about the lengths of their sides and the sizes of their angles.
- If you are asked to draw a 2D shape in your Maths National Test, you will be expected to use a ruler and a protractor to do it.

Use sheets of plain paper to draw shapes in this chapter.

A 2D shape is drawn on a flat surface. Always use a sharp pencil and a ruler to draw shapes.

Vertical means straight up. A 90° angle is called a right angle. A square has four equal sides and four right angles.

1 Draw a horizontal line 5 cm long.

Place the protractor with the middle of its base line on the end of the line. Mark an angle of 90°.

Draw a vertical line 5 cm long.

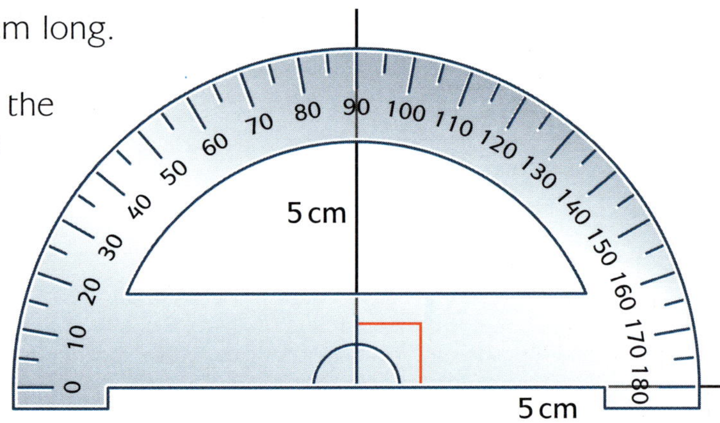

Measure another angle of 90° at the other end of the line.

Draw another vertical line 5 cm long.

Check the 90° angles and join up the square.

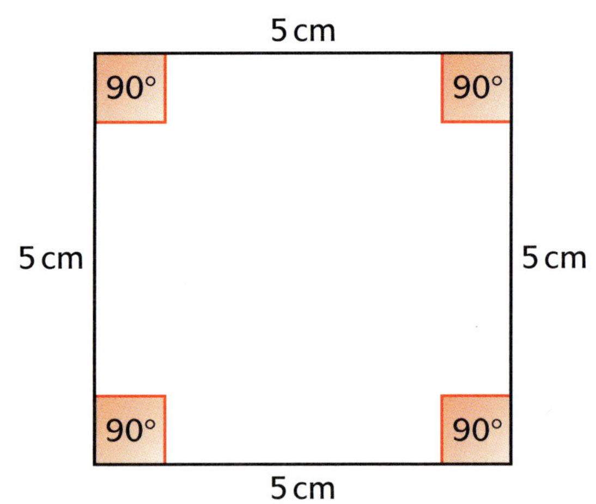

2 Use a protractor to measure the marked angles.

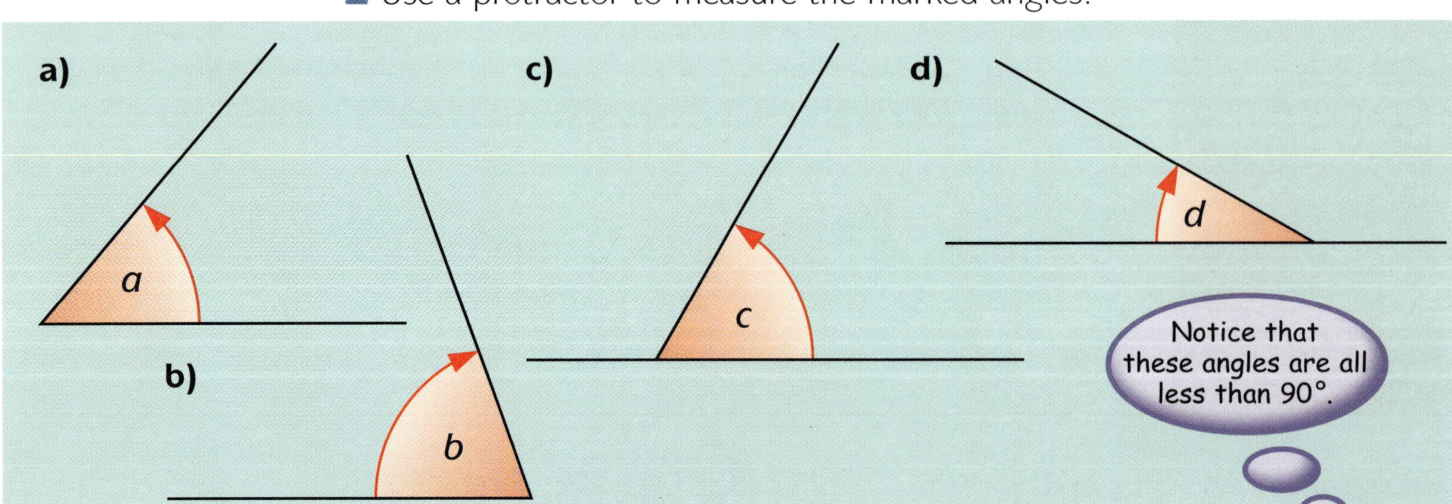

Notice that these angles are all less than 90°.

An equilateral triangle has three sides all the same length and three angles all equal to 60°.

Remember to use the correct scale on the protractor.

An isosceles triangle has two equal sides and two equal angles.

3 Draw an equilateral triangle like this.

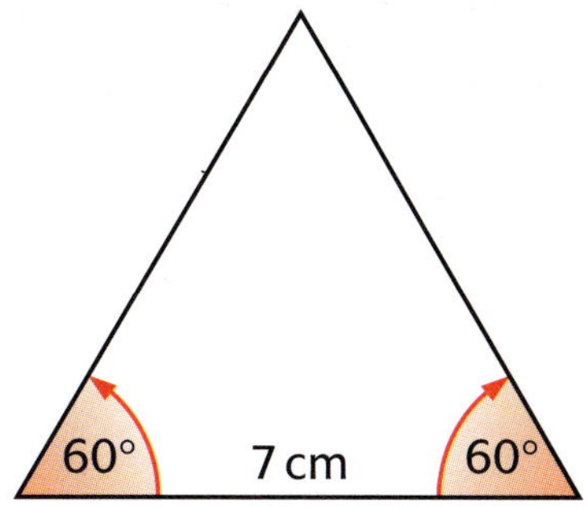

Draw a line 7 cm long.

Place the protractor with the middle of its base line on one end of the line.

Mark 60°.

Repeat the angle measurement at the other end of the line.

Check that the lines are 7 cm long and each of the angles is 60°.

4 Draw an isosceles triangle like this.

Draw a line 6 cm long.

Measure and draw angles of 70° at the ends of the line.

Complete the isosceles triangle.

What is the length of the equal sides? ______________________

5 Copy and complete these drawings of squares and triangles. Use a separate piece of paper.

a)

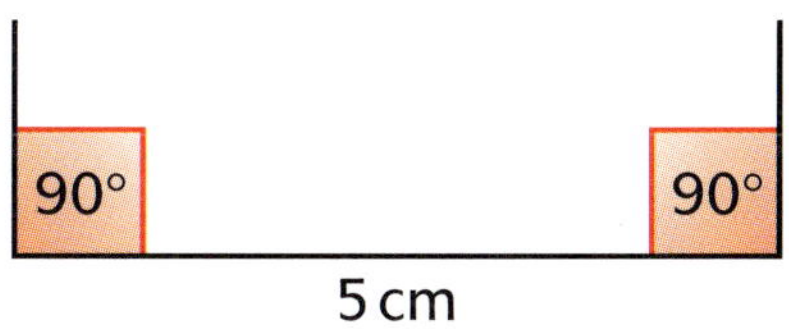

____

c)

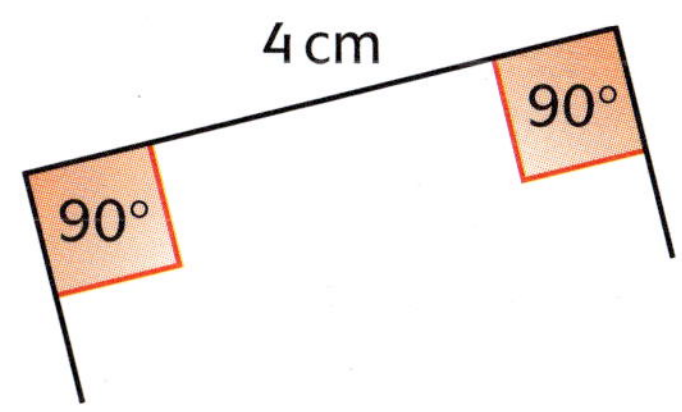

____

b)

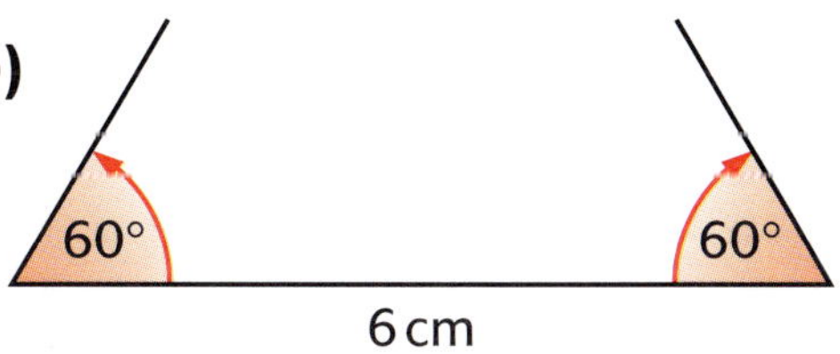

____

d)

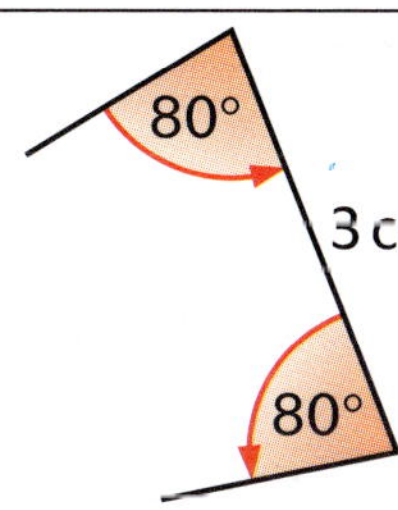

____

Name each of the shapes you have drawn.

Test question

Use a ruler to draw **two more lines** to make an isosceles triangle.

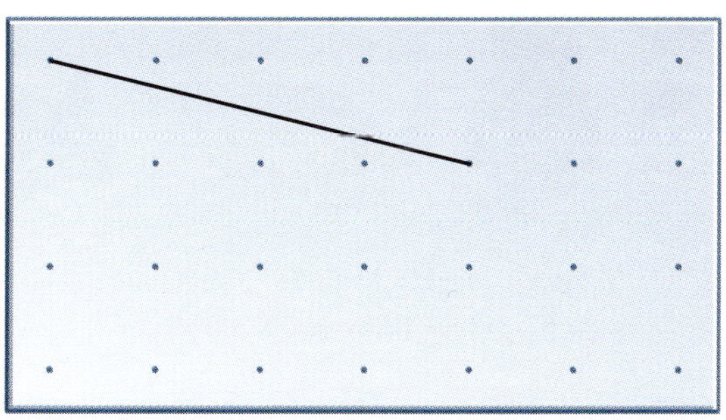

Answers and Guidance are given on pp.37-38.

How long did you take?

4 Missing numbers

What's it all about?

- In this chapter you will look at the ways that adding and subtracting are linked to each other.
- In your Maths National Test you may be asked to find missing numbers. To do this you may need to use your knowledge of how addition and subtraction are linked.
- You should also use this knowledge to check your answer to any addition or subtraction sum that you do.

> Look carefully at the numbers in each pair of sums. Are they the same? What are you doing that links them together? Try to write down exactly what is happening.

1 Put the missing signs in the boxes.

Look carefully at how each sum is linked to the other in the pair.

a) 6 ☐ 4 = 2 and 2 ☐ 4 = 6

b) 9 ☐ 2 = 7 and 7 ☐ 2 = 9

c) 4 ☐ 9 = 13 and 13 ☐ 9 = 4

d) 24 ☐ 14 = 10 and 10 ☐ 14 = 24

What do you notice about each pair of sums?

> If you are not sure that you can do the sum in your head, try first – but then check by writing it down.

2 Now use what you have learned to help you to do these. Try doing them in your head first.

____ – 4 = 12 You can do this by rewriting it as 12 + 4 = 16.

____ + 26 = 84 You can do this by rewriting it as 84 – 26 = 58.

Or you might want to write it like this:

$$\begin{array}{r} 84 \\ -\underline{26} \\ \underline{58} \end{array}$$

a) ____ + 5 = 55	**g)** ____ – 23 = 87
b) ____ – 8 = 17	**h)** ____ + 56 = 99
c) ____ + 7 = 26	**i)** ____ + 93 = 105
d) ____ – 13 = 29	**j)** ____ – 125 = 294
e) ____ + 16 = 42	**k)** ____ – 123 = 567
f) ____ – 34 = 45	**l)** ____ + 335 = 673

> It's good practice to work these out but you could check them with a calculator.

> It is often easier to do a sum written vertically, e.g. $\begin{array}{r} 92 \\ -\underline{76} \\ \underline{16} \end{array}$

3 Now try these.

76 + ____ = 92 You can do them by rewriting each sum like this: 92 – 76 = 16.

a) 29 + ____ = 67	**e)** 283 + ____ = 431
b) 76 + ____ = 81	**f)** 543 + ____ = 678
c) 66 + ____ = 93	**g)** 615 + ____ = 1029
d) 96 + ____ = 179	**h)** 1542 + ____ = 2347

Always check your answers by looking at the whole sum, to see if what you have written makes sense.

4 Now answer these.

57 – ____ = 24 You can do this by writing it as 57 – 24 = 33

or if it is easier

```
  57
– 24
  33
```

a) 78 – ____ = 64
b) 92 – ____ =71
c) 62 – ____ = 43
d) 157 – ____ = 129
e) 724 – ____ = 352
f) 985 – ____ = 657
g) 980 – ____ = 365
h) 1198 – ____ = 1076

Some of these may be tricky to do in your head! Check by writing them down.

5 These sums are mixed. Think carefully!

a) ____ + 46 = 83
b) 21 + ____ = 80
c) 198 – ____ = 128
d) 1348 + ____ = 2371
e) ____ – 1138 = 978
f) ____ – 164 = 547
g) 4672 – ____ = 2398
h) 9856 – ____ = 5382
i) ____ + 51 290 = 72 549
j) 654 + ____ = 879

You can use what you have learned on these pages to check your answers to other addition and subtraction sums.

6 Calculate the answers to these questions and then write another sum to check your answer. The first is done for you.

a) 672 + 82 = 754 Check: 754 – 82 = 672
b) 52 + 34 = ____ Check: ________
c) 82 – 58 = ____ Check: ________
d) 186 – 145 = ____ Check: ________
e) 879 – 451 = ____ Check: ________
f) 587 + 326 = ____ Check: ________

Test question

Write the missing numbers.

[ ] + 79 = 191 260 – [ ] = 126

Answers and Guidance are given on pp.38-39. *How long did you take?*

National Test Questions 1

You should be able to complete these questions in 6–10 minutes.

1 Raj thinks of a number.

He says, 'If I subtract 14 from it, I get 29.'

What is Raj's number?

....

1 mark

2 Use a ruler to draw an equilateral triangle on this circle.

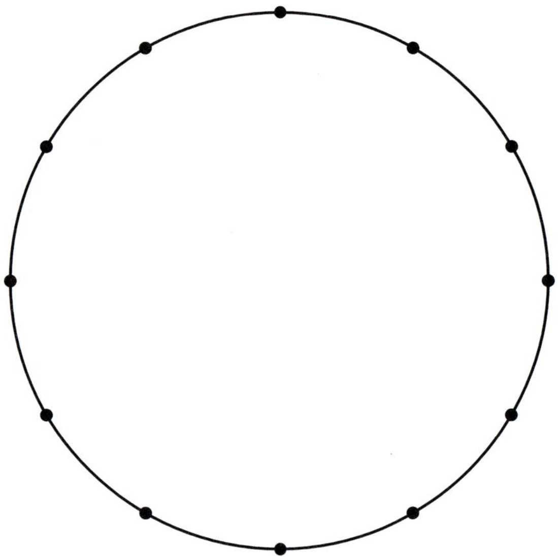

1 mark

3 Write the missing numbers in these sequences.

6 10 14 11 8 12 16 13 ☐ ☐

66 ☐ 50 42 ☐ 26 18

1 mark

National Test Questions 1

4

Weston Castle

Opening Times

	July 1st to August 31st	September 1st to June 30th
Monday to Friday	10 a.m. – 7 p.m.	closed
Saturday and Sunday	9 a.m. – 8 p.m.	1 p.m. – 5 p.m.

At what time does the castle close on Wednesday July 15th?

....

1 mark

For which months is the castle open seven days a week?

....

1 mark

On Sunday March 8th John goes into the castle at 3 p.m.
He stays until closing time.

For how many hours does he stay in the castle?

....

1 mark

Answers and Guidance are given on p.46.

How long did you take?

5 Using multiplication

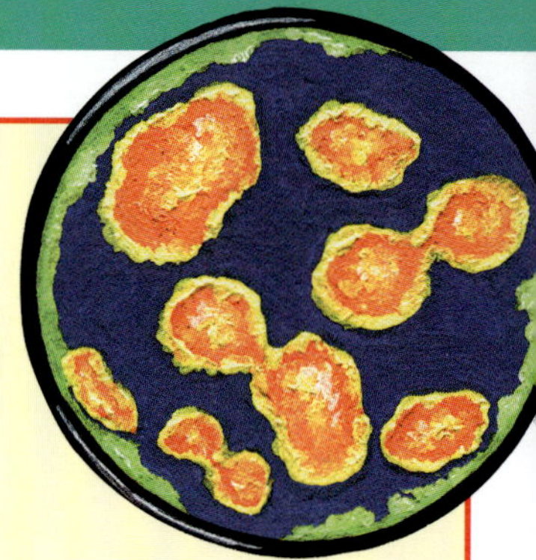

What's it all about?

- The questions in this chapter give you a chance to practise multiplying numbers in a lot of different ways.
- To answer the questions, you need to think about how to use what you probably already know about multiplication.
- Your Maths National Test will expect you to use what you know about multiplication.

Zero multiplied by any number is still zero so: 2345 × 0 = 0 0 × 5 = 0

1 Complete each group as quickly as you can.

a)		**b)**		**c)**		**d)**	
	9 × 6 = ___		7 × 0 = ___		8 × 7 = ___		6 × 9 = ___
	8 × 9 = ___		10 × 7 = ___		9 × 8 = ___		6 × 8 = ___
	9 × 9 = ___		7 × 5 = ___		3 × 8 = ___		5 × 6 = ___
	4 × 9 = ___		7 × 8 = ___		0 × 8 = ___		6 × 6 = ___
	3 × 9 = ___		9 × 7 = ___		8 × 8 = ___		3 × 6 = ___
	9 × 5 = ___		6 × 7 = ___		8 × 4 = ___		7 × 6 = ___

The numbers you have circled are called **factors** of the number on the left, e.g. 5 and 7 are factors of 35.

2 The numbers in the left-hand column are in the times-tables of some of the numbers in the rows. **Circle** these numbers. The first one is done for you.

35	2	3	4	5	6	7	8	9	10	11	12
48	2	3	4	5	6	7	8	9	10	11	12
36	2	3	4	5	6	7	8	9	10	11	12
60	2	3	4	5	6	7	8	9	10	11	12
28	2	3	4	5	6	7	8	9	10	11	12
54	2	3	4	5	6	7	8	9	10	11	12

Notice that some numbers fit into more than one group.

3 Number search.

Put a **line** through all the numbers that can be divided by 7.

Put a **circle** round all the numbers that can be divided by 6.

Put a **box** round all the numbers that can be divided by 8.

56	45	30	72	18	16	21	57	66	80
39	35	48	63	14	42	28	44	70	32
27	54	24	36	40	60	49	12	64	50

4 For each of these sums, write the number that is one less than the answer. The first two have been done for you.

a)	6 × 6	35	**f)**	8 × 2	___
b)	4 × 4	15	**g)**	5 × 9	___
c)	9 × 3	___	**h)**	2 × 7	___
d)	7 × 5	___	**i)**	10 × 3	___
e)	3 × 8	___	**j)**	9 × 1	___

5 Try these. The first two have been done for you.

The multiples are in the times-table of the given number.

a) Circle the multiples of 6.

(24) 26 (30) (42) 44 50 (60)

b) Circle the numbers that are 2 more than a multiple of 6.

24 (26) 30 34 (44) (50) 60

Now do these.

c) Circle the multiples of 7.

13 49 35 29 46 55 56

d) Circle the numbers that are 2 more than a multiple of 7.

16 26 37 40 41 51 59

e) Circle the numbers that are 2 more than a multiple of 9.

20 25 38 47 51 66 79

f) Circle the numbers that are 2 more than a multiple of 4.

17 24 26 29 30 33 46

If you find these difficult, write out the table of the given number (its multiples). Then add 2 to each multiple and see if any of the numbers you get are in the row of numbers you are given.

6 Answer these questions.

a) Write three **multiples** of 9. ____________________

b) Write four **factors** of 40. ____________________

c) Write a number that, when **multiplied by itself**, gives the answer 64.

____

d) Write three numbers that can be divided by 6 **without remainder**.

____

e) Write five **factors** of 30. ____________________

Make sure you know what each of the maths words means.

Test question

A number multiplied by itself gives the answer 49.

Circle the number.

2 3 4 5 6 7 8 9

Answers and Guidance are given on pp.39–40.

How long did you take?

6 Number lines and scales

What's it all about?

- ★ You see metric units used in many places – on rulers, tape measures, weighing scales and measuring jugs.
- ★ This chapter helps you practise reading and writing number lines and scales, using metric units.
- ★ In your Maths National Test you may be expected to use quite large numbers on number lines or scales.

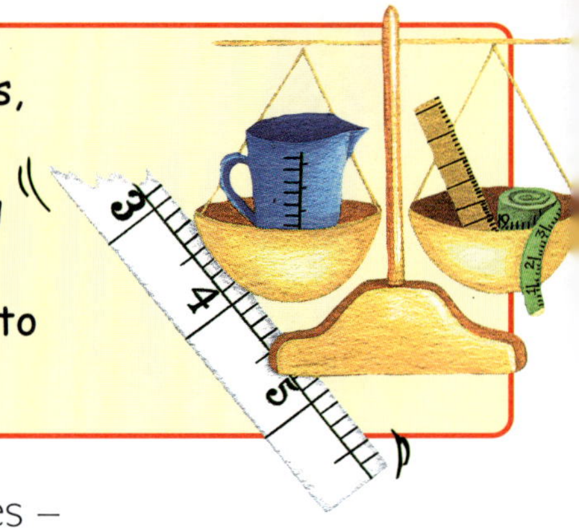

1 Mark these measurements on the number lines – the first one has been done for you.

cm = centimetre
mm = millimetre

a) cm

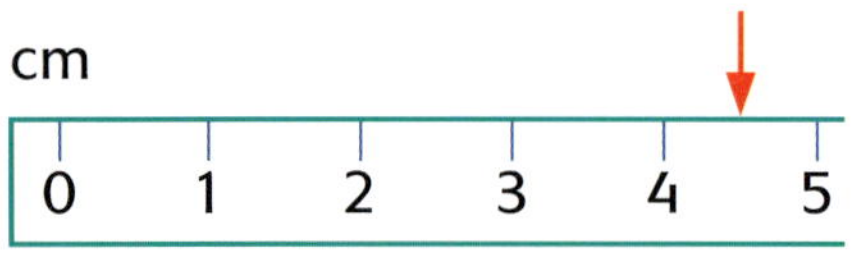

Mark $4\frac{1}{2}$ cm.

c) cm

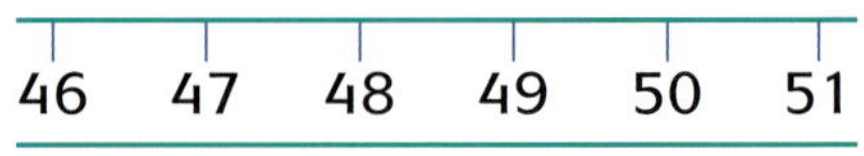

Mark $49\frac{1}{2}$ cm.

b) mm

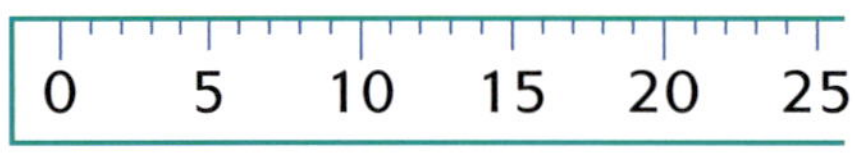

Mark 12 mm.

d) mm

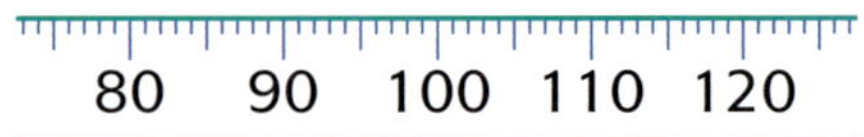

Mark 103 mm.

2 On these scales, you need to decide what each division means before you count. Complete the scales – the first one has been done for you.

When we measure weight (or mass) we use weighing scales or balance weights.

g = gram
kg = kilogram

a) g

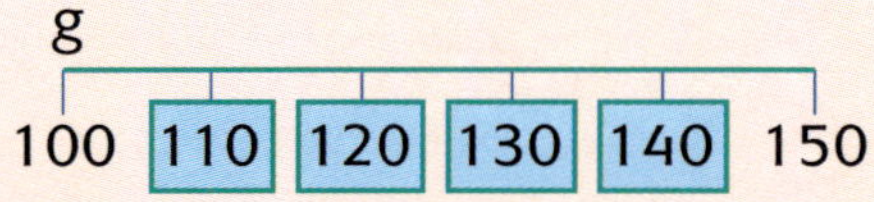

d) g

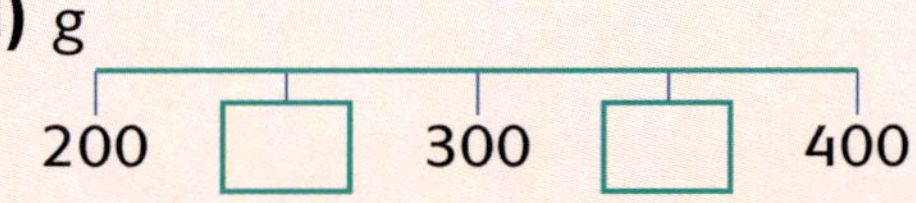

b) kg

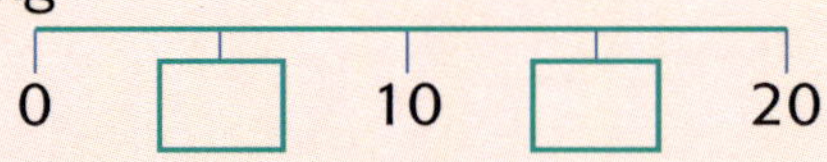

e) g

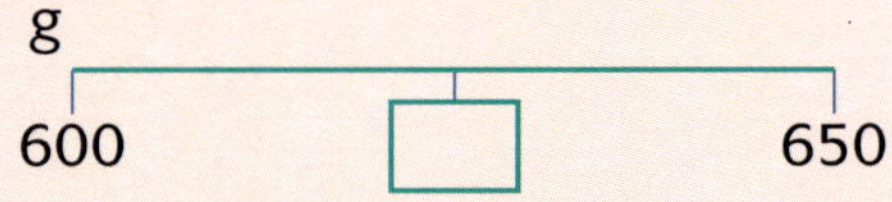

c) kg

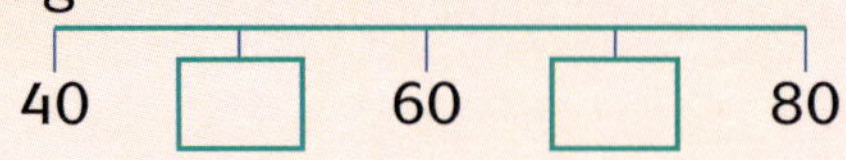

f) g

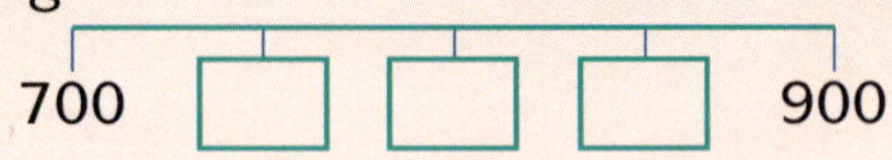

3 Write down the measurements shown by the arrows.

The divisions on a number line or scale are always equal in size. Some scales may have large divisions that are marked with smaller divisions. Sometimes the scales go up in 5s, sometimes in 10s, 50s, 100s ...

a) g

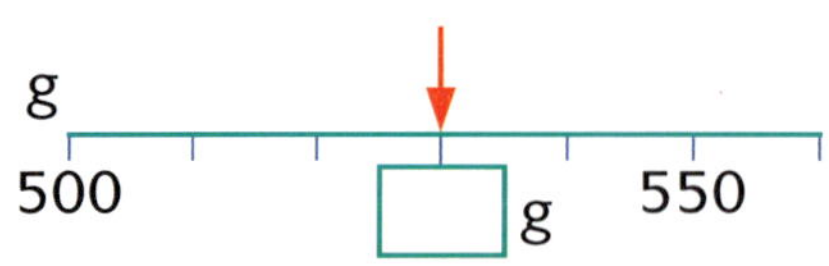

c) kg

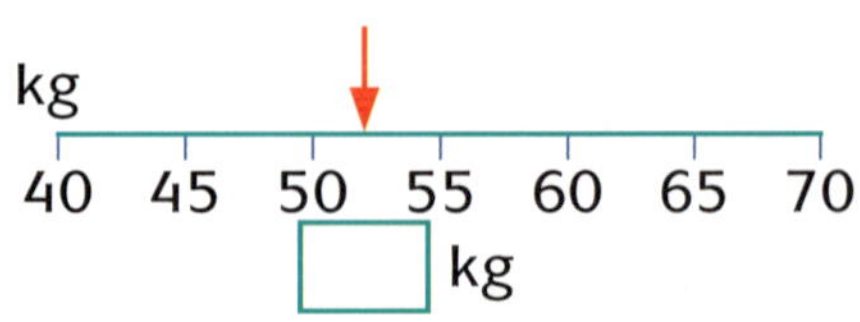

b) g

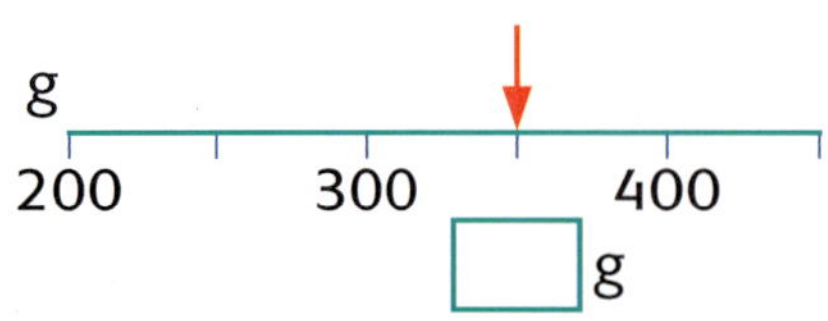

d) kg

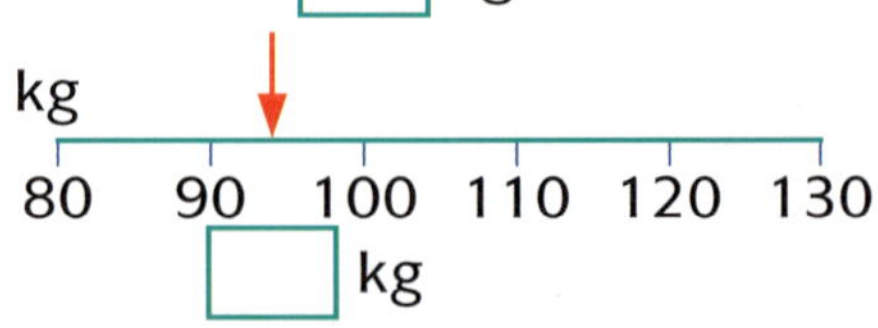

4 Mark the divisions on these scales.

a) cm

900 ☐ 1100 ☐ ☐ ☐ 1500

b) km

500 ☐ 1500 ☐ 2500

c) mm

1000 ☐ ☐ ☐ ☐ 2000

d) kg

2000 ☐ ☐ ☐ 10 000

You can use an arrow or a cross. Whichever you use, make sure you mark the point clearly.

5 Mark these points on the number lines.

a) 800 — 900

Mark 860.

b) 750 — 850

Mark 770 and 840.

c) 300 — 500

Mark 360 and 460.

d) 1000 — 1100

Mark 1020 and 1110.

Test question

Here is part of a number line.

Write in the number indicated by the arrow.

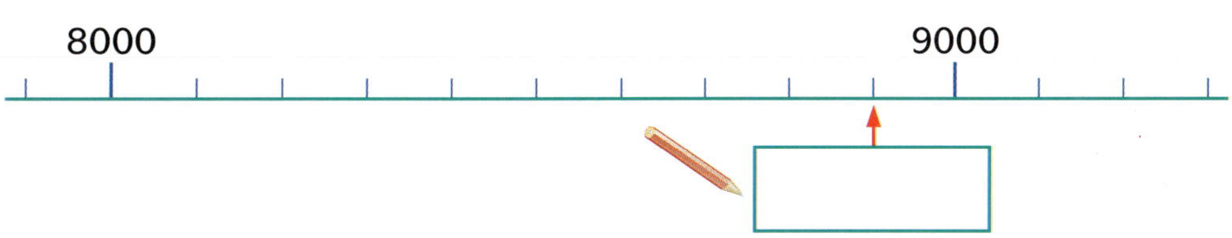

Answers and Guidance are given on pp.40–41.

How long did you take?

7 Probability

What's it all about?

- This chapter explains some of the words that are used to talk about probability.
- You will need to understand and use these words in some National Test questions that ask you about probability.

1

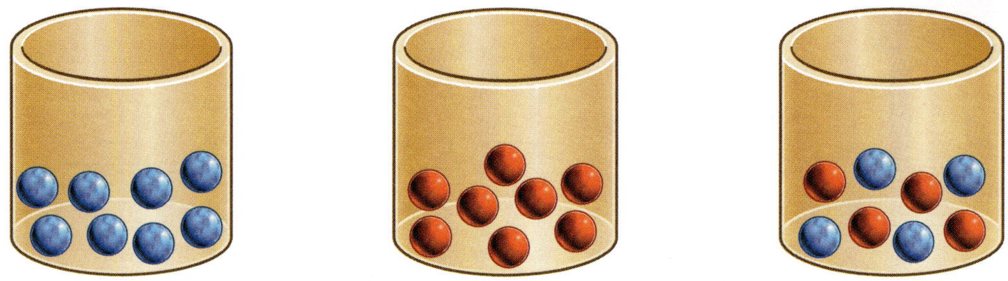

A **B** **C**

a) I am certain of taking a blue marble out of pot A. True or false?

b) It is impossible to take a blue marble out of pot B. True or false?

c) There is an even chance of getting a red marble from pot C. True or false?

d) From which pot would I be certain to take a red marble? ____

e) From which pot have I an even chance of taking a blue marble? ____

2

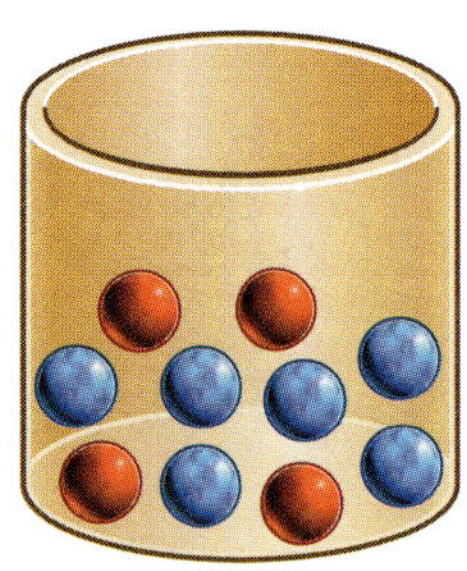

What is the chance of getting a blue marble?

certain	impossible	likely	even	unlikely

3 It is likely that a marble taken from this pot will be blue. Can you explain why?

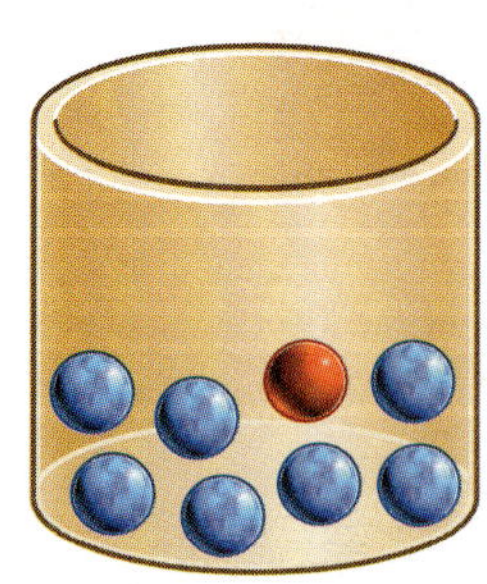

____

____

____

Look at the spinner carefully. What numbers could you score? How many different numbers could you score? What numbers could you not score?

4 Look at this spinner.

Use the words from the box to answer the following questions.

impossible	likely	unlikely
certain	an even chance	

If I spin the spinner just once, how likely is it that I will score:

a) 12 ________________

b) an odd number ________________

c) a number under 9 ________________

d) a number over 9 ________________

e) a number under 11? ________________

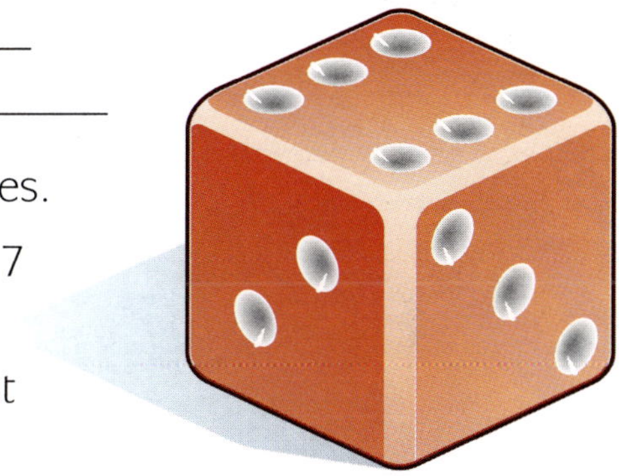

5 Think about a dice. Finish these sentences.

a) It is ________________ to score a 7 in one throw.

b) I am ________________ to score at least a total of 2 in two throws.

c) I am ________________ to score five 6s in a row.

d) I am ________________ to score a number less than 5 next throw.

e) There is ________________ of scoring a 3 or less next throw.

Test question

Mel uses an eight-sided spinner.

Draw lines to show how **likely** the following scores are.

a number less than 10	impossible
the number 11	unlikely
the same number three times in a row	even chance
an odd number	likely
	certain

Answers and Guidance are given on p.41.

How long did you take?

8 Perimeters

What's it all about?

- This chapter reminds you how to work out the perimeters of shapes with straight sides.
- It also reminds you how to draw a shape with a perimeter of a particular length.
- Your Maths National Test may include a question that asks you to do either of these two things.

1 Let's begin by looking at some shapes made with centimetre squares.

The distance around the outside edge of this shape (its **perimeter**) is 4 centimetres.

Look at this shape.

What is the perimeter measurement of the shape?

We can find the answer by counting the number of centimetres around the shape.

It doesn't matter which way round you number or count the squares.

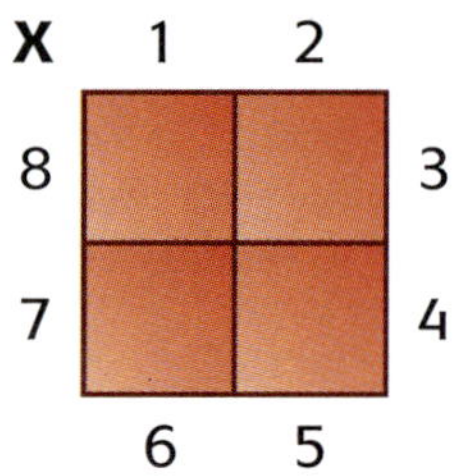

From **X** we count each centimetre square in turn. It helps to write the numbers in, like this.

So the perimeter of the shape is 8 cm.

2 Find the perimeter of each of these shapes.

To help you keep track, use a **X** to show where to start to count and write in the numbers.

a)

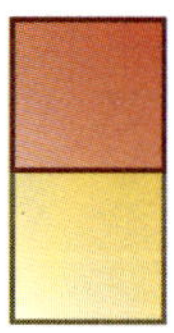

______

c)

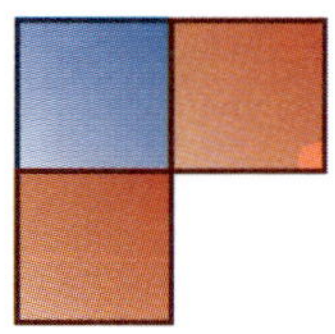

______

e)

______

b)

______

d)

______

f)

______

There are lots of different ways of arranging squares. The way you arrange them can affect the perimeter. Look at these ways of arranging four squares.

perimeter 8

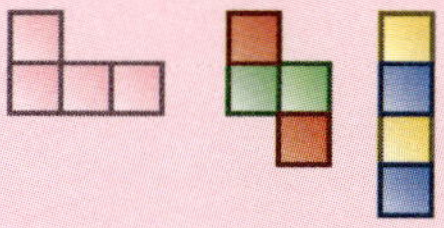

perimeter 10

You will need centimetre dotted paper or squared paper for this page.

3 a) What is the perimeter of this 1 centimetre square? ____________

b) What is the perimeter when you add another centimetre square? ____________

c) Write down the perimeter of shapes made with:

i) 4 centimetre squares ______

ii) 5 centimetre squares ______

iii) 6 centimetre squares ______

d) Now add on more squares and calculate the perimeter measurement of your shapes.

4 Sometimes you need to be able to draw shapes which have a particular perimeter. Draw some shapes with these perimeters. Use centimetre dotted paper or squared paper.

a) 10 cm	**c)** 14 cm	**e)** 20 cm
b) 12 cm	**d)** 6 cm	**f)** 16 cm

Test question

These shapes are all made with centimetre squares.

A

B

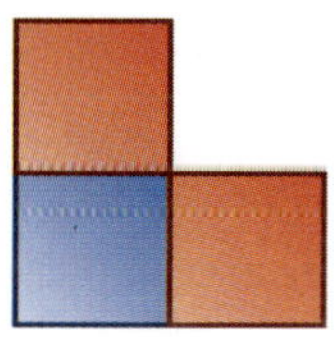

C

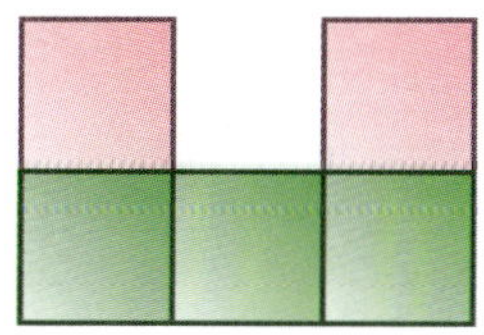

D

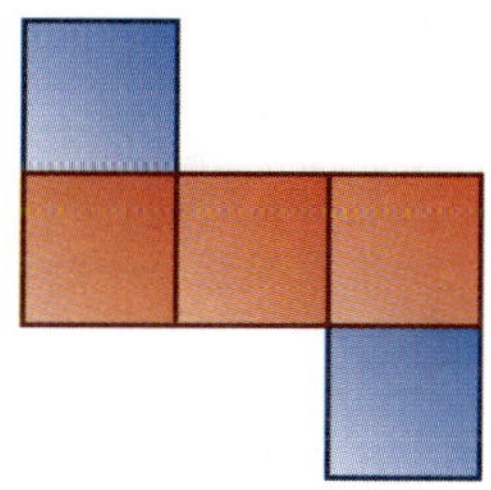

E

F

G

H

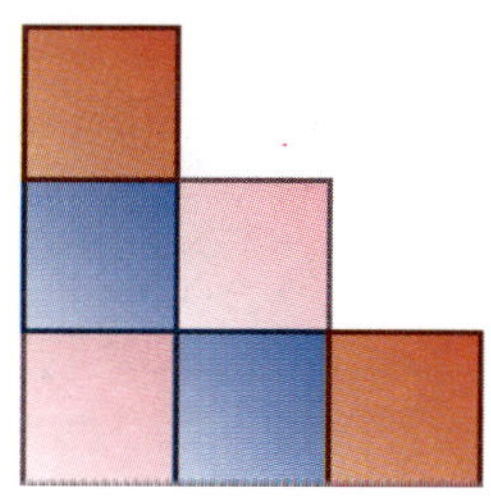

Which shape has a perimeter of 10 cm?

____

Answers and Guidance are given on pp.41–42.

How long did you take?

National Test Questions 2

You should be able to complete these questions in 5–8 minutes.

1 This piece of cheese has a mass of 350 grams.

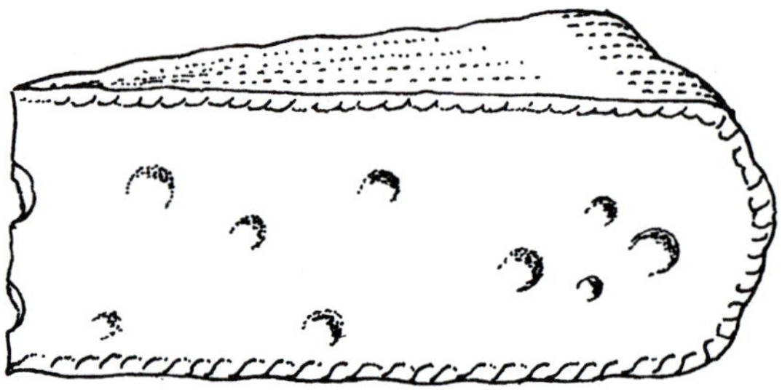

Draw an arrow (↓) on the scale to show the reading for 350 g.

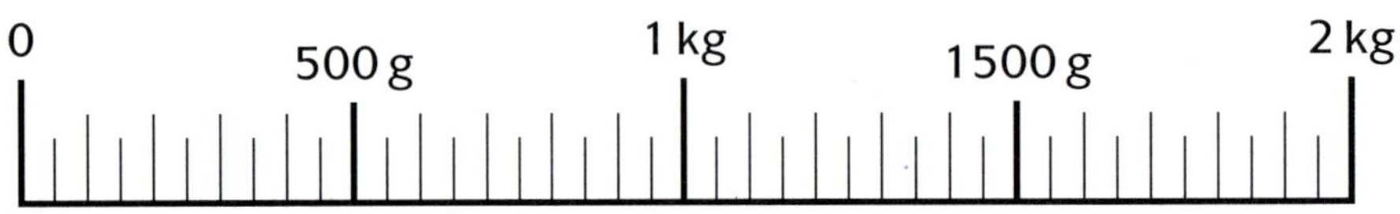

1 mark

2 On the grid below, draw a rectangle which has a perimeter of 10 centimetres.

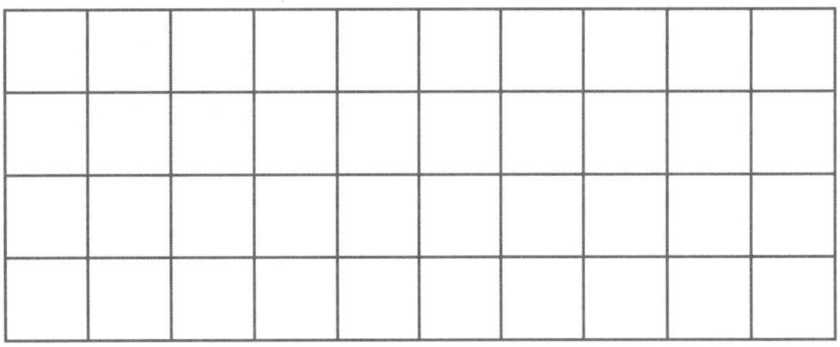

1 mark

3 Circle one number in the grid which can be divided by 9, leaving a remainder of 1.

97	98	99
107	108	109
117	118	119

1 mark

National Test Questions 2

4 Barry keeps six pairs of football socks in a drawer.

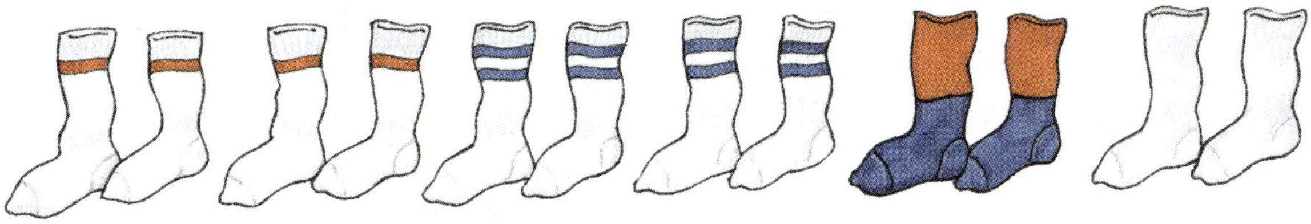

Two pairs are white with red stripes, two pairs are white with blue stripes, one pair is red and blue, one pair is all white.

Barry chooses a pair without looking. Draw lines to show the chances.

What is the chance that Barry chooses:

a pair of socks with white in them	certain
a pair without white in them	likely
a pair of yellow socks	even chance
a pair of socks	unlikely
a pair with blue in them	impossible

1 mark

Answers and Guidance are given on pp.46-47. ***How long did you take?***

9 Using bar graphs

What's it all about?

- ★ Information that is collected by counting or measuring can be recorded on a bar graph.
- ★ Bar graphs are one way in which data are recorded.
- ★ This chapter gives you practice in drawing and interpreting bar graphs.

1 This table shows the numbers of vehicles which passed a school during one hour.

Cars	85
Lorries	20
Vans	40
Bicycles	105
Motor bikes	25

A graph should always have a title. You should also write down what information is being shown on each axis.

Draw a bar graph of this information.
The first two types of vehicle have been done for you.

Title: The number of different types of vehicle which passed the school in one hour

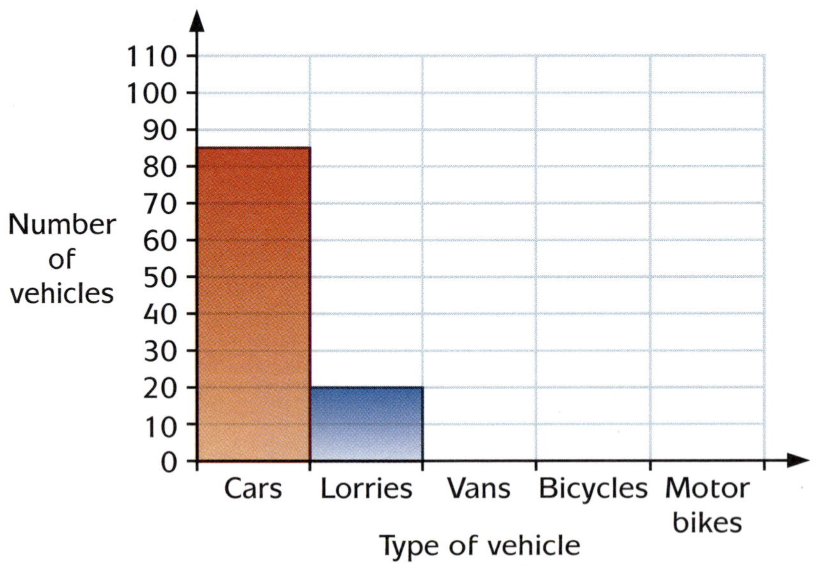

The line that goes up the page is called the **vertical axis** and the line that goes across the page is called the **horizontal axis**.

If you have difficulty with the scale on the vertical axis, look back to the section about reading scales, on pages 16–17.

Now answer these questions about the graph you have drawn.

a) How many more cars than vans went past the school? ____________

b) Which type of vehicle passed least often? ____________

c) Which types of vehicle passed more than 60 times? ____________

d) How many vehicles passed the school altogether? ____________

e) How many two-wheeled vehicles passed altogether? ____________

In the bar graph in question 1 the bars were drawn up the paper. You can also draw bar graphs with the bars across the paper, as in question 2.

Notice that the numbers on a bar chart are placed on the lines, not between the lines.

Sometimes a bar graph is called a bar chart – it means the same thing.

2 This graph shows the type of weather recorded each day for a whole year. Give it a suitable title.

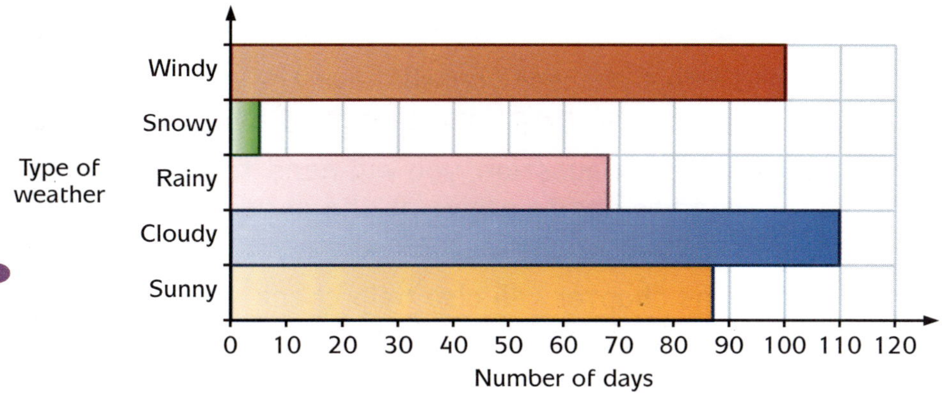

a) How many more days were sunny than snowy? ________

b) How many days were either cloudy or windy? ________

c) Which type of weather was seen on fewer than 20 days? ________

d) Which types of weather were seen on more than 90 days? ________

3 This table shows how many children stay to school lunch on each day.

Monday	*Tuesday*	*Wednesday*	*Thursday*	*Friday*
120	*80*	*90*	*110*	*100*

On centimetre squared paper, draw a bar chart from the information. Use a set of axes like this. Remember to give it a title.

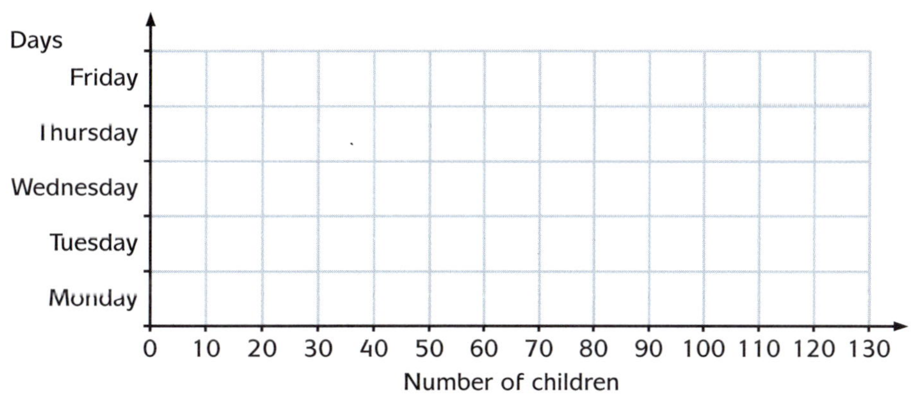

Test question

Here are some long jump results.

Sue jumped **212 cm**.

Draw Sue's long jump result on the graph.

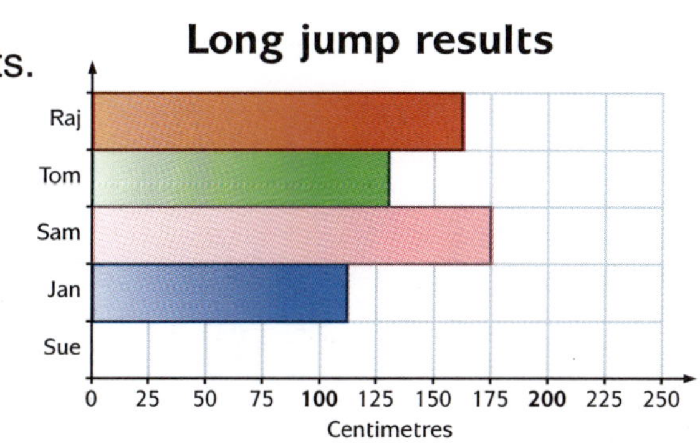

Answers and Guidance are given on pp.42–43.

How long did you take?

10 Solving problems

What's it all about?

- ★ In this chapter you will have the chance to solve a number of different kinds of maths problems.
- ★ For each question, you will need to decide what methods you need to use to arrive at the answer. You must always think carefully whether the answer you find makes sense.
- ★ This chapter will also help check your understanding of maths language.
- ★ Your Maths National Test will include several problem-solving questions where you have to decide how to answer them.

To solve a problem successfully, you must read the question very carefully and think what it means.

1 Check that you understand maths language by solving these problems.

a) What is the sum of 3, 5, 7 and 9? ____________

b) What is the difference between 46 and 78? ____________

c) What is the total of 6, 17, 32 and 12? ____________

d) What number is 15 smaller than 78? ____________

e) What is the product of 4 and 5? ____________

f) How many more than 56 is 79? ____________

g) What number is 33 fewer than 76? ____________

h) Write three numbers which are divisible by 4. ____________

When you are given a problem, ask yourself, 'What maths do I need to use?'

2 Write the maths that you need to use to solve these problems – then solve them. The first problem is done for you.

a) There are 215 children at North Road School, This is 37 more than there are at South Lane School. How many children go to South Lane?

Working (maths needed): 215 − 37

Answer: 178

Read the question twice before you start. Make sure you know what you are being asked to do!

b) The difference in age between Annie and Mary is 13 years. Mary is 51.

Annie is older than Mary. How old is Annie?

Working:

Answer:

You should always show your working – you may get marks even if you make a mistake.

c) Ten children in Class 5 at St Mary's School are 9 years old. Seventeen are 10 years old. What is the sum of their ages?

Working:

Answer:

Don't forget to make the units clear when giving your answers.

When solving problems, getting the units right is just as important as doing the sums correctly, e.g. 9 grams and 9 kilograms.

3 a) How much is the total cost of 1 sausage, 1 burger and 2 bags of chips?

Working:

Answer:

Chip Shop Prices

Cod	£1.20
Sausage	50p
Burger	£1.10
Chips	60p
Fish and chips	£1.50
Burger and chips	£1.70

b) What is the difference between the cost of fish and chips and the cost of a piece of cod and a bag of chips?

Working:

Answer:

4 A package weighs 36 grams less than a parcel. The parcel weighs 99 grams.
How much does the package weigh?

Working:

Answer:

5 It costs £3.10 for one child to go to the museum on a coach. It is 50p for each child to go into the museum. The Bowley twins want to go on the outing. How much will it cost for them both to go?

Working:

Answer:

Test question

Jill orders one small cheese pizza with extra tomato.

What is the total cost?

Ben buys one small pizza and one medium pizza.
They cost him £10.

Which two could they be?

One small __________ pizza

and one medium __________ pizza

Pizzas

	small	medium
Ham	£4.20	£5.50
Salami	£4.40	£5.75
Mushroom	£4.50	£6.00
Cheese	£3.80	£4.95
Tuna	£4.25	£5.40

Extra tomato 50p
Extra cheese 60p

Answers and Guidance are given on p.43.

How long did you take?

11 Reflective symmetry

What's it all about?

- When a shape is folded in half and both sides are exactly the same, then the shape has reflective symmetry.
- This chapter shows you how to use a mirror line to work out whether shapes have reflective symmetry.

You will need:
- paper
- ruler
- sharp pencil
- mirror
- tracing paper.

1 Draw a square on a piece of paper, then draw a diagonal line on the square.

Place a mirror on the diagonal line.

What do you see?

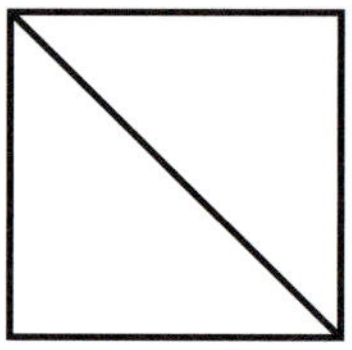

You should have seen an exact copy of the triangle – the triangle on the paper and its **reflection** should look like the original square.

2 Place a mirror on the line through each of the shapes below.
Tick the shapes that have reflective symmetry.

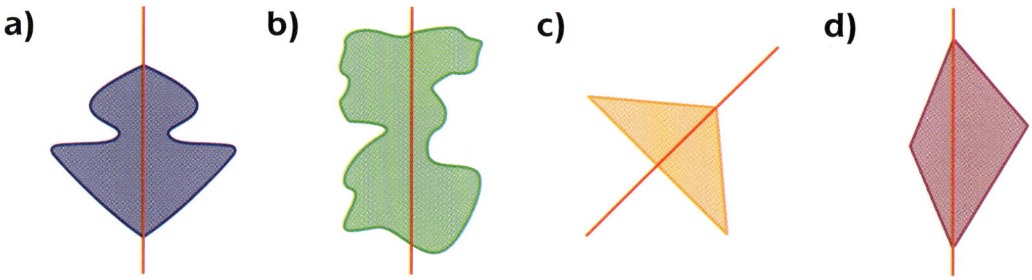

The line through the shapes that have reflective symmetry is called the **mirror line**.

3 Draw mirror lines on the shapes that have reflective symmetry.

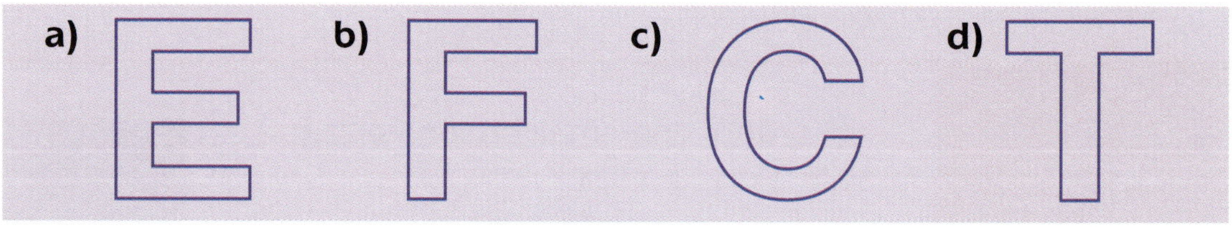

4 Trace this shape onto tracing paper.

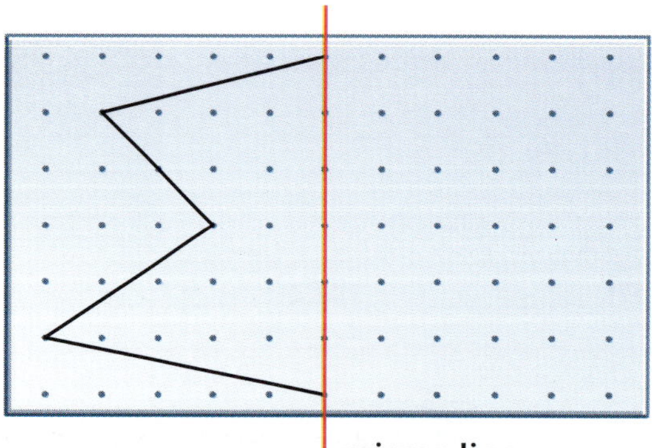

Turn the tracing paper over and line up the mirror line on the page with the one on your tracing. Go over the tracing. The shape you have drawn is the reflection of the original shape.

You could use dotted paper instead of tracing paper. Instead of tracing, count the dots from the mirror line.

You can use either tracing or dotted paper. Remember to use a sharp pencil.

5 Now do the same with these.

a)

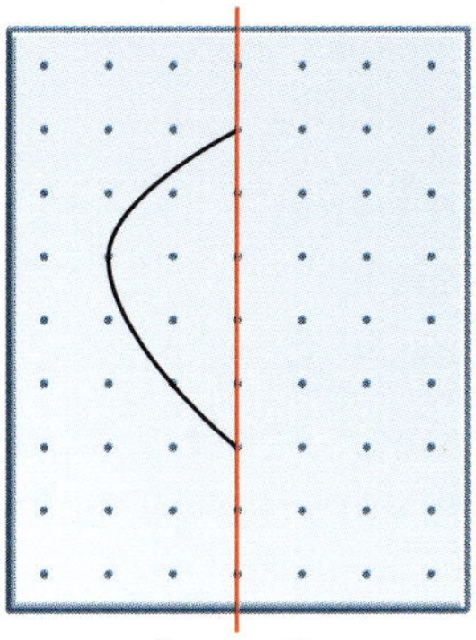

mirror line

b)

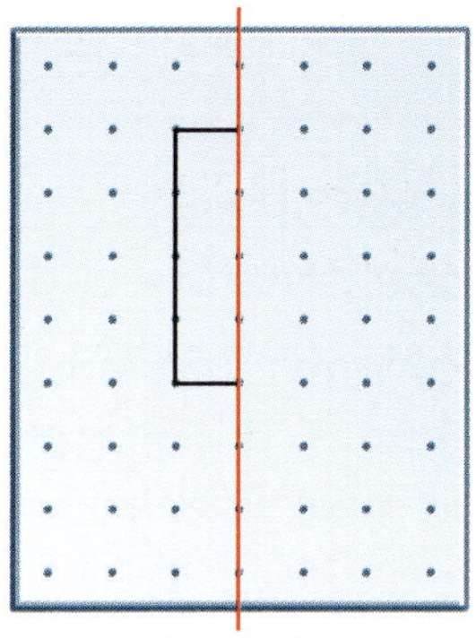

mirror line

c)

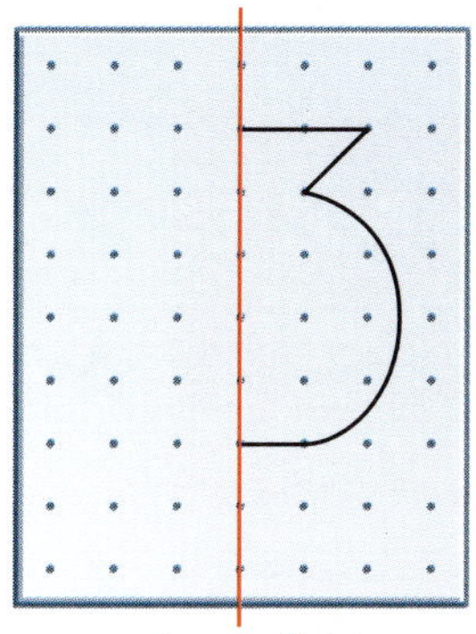

mirror line

Remember that the letters can have a mirror line across as well as down, from top to bottom.

6 Mark all the capital letters of the alphabet that have reflective symmetry.

A B C D E F G H I

J K L M N O P Q R

S T U V W X Y Z

Test question

Draw the reflection of this triangle in the mirror line.

You may use a ruler.

You may use tracing paper.

Counting the dots may help you.

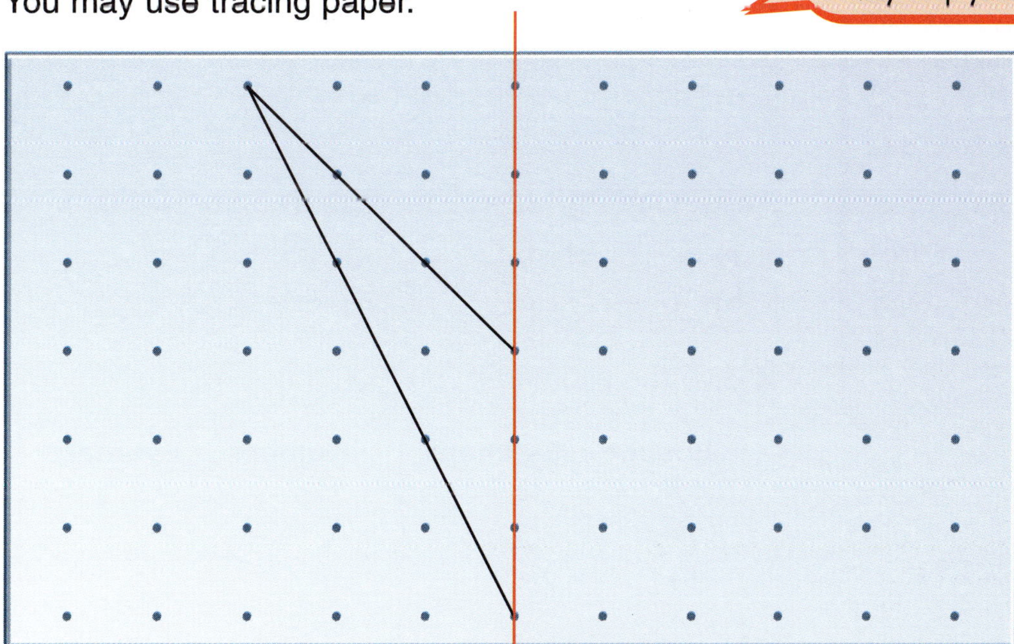

mirror line

Answers and Guidance are given on p.44.

How long did you take?

12 Using a calculator

What's it all about?

- This chapter gives you practice in using a calculator sensibly and accurately.
- It is important that you are able to use a calculator as it can help you answer some types of questions more quickly. It also lets you work with very large numbers more easily.
- In Test B of your Maths National Test, you are allowed to use a calculator. You need to use it as it will help you do the questions quickly so that you finish the paper.

It is very easy to make mistakes when you use a calculator.

≈ means 'equals approximately'.

You need to be able to check that the answer you get is sensible. In order to do this, you need to have some idea of the type of answer you are expecting.

1 Make estimates for these calculations **without** using your calculator.
The first one has been done for you.

For numbers less than 100, round up or down to the nearest 10. If the last digit is 5 or more, round up. If it is 4 or less, round down, e.g. 17 becomes 20 and 12 becomes 10.
Between 100 and 1000 it is sensible to estimate to the nearest 50 or 100, e.g. 340 becomes 350 and 760 becomes 750.

a) 17 + 12 is approximately 20 + 10 = 30 so 17 + 12 ≈ 30
b) 96 + 31 is approximately ___ + ___ = ___ so 96 + 31 ≈ ___
c) 68 + 53 is approximately ___ + ___ = ___ so 68 + 53 ≈ ___
d) 84 + 12 is approximately ___ + ___ = ___ so 84 + 12 ≈ ___
e) 55 + 34 is approximately ___ + ___ = ___ so 55 + 34 ≈ ___
f) 21 + 78 is approximately ___ + ___ = ___ so 21 + 78 ≈ ___

Now find the actual answers using a calculator.

a) 17 + 12 = ___ **c)** 68 + 53 = ___ **e)** 55 + 34 = ___
b) 96 + 31 = ___ **d)** 84 + 12 = ___ **f)** 21 + 78 = ___

2 Give the estimates you would use for these numbers.

Number	Estimate
17	20
607	600
730	750
914	
107	
24	
999	

Number	Estimate
225	
89	
467	
855	
775	
25	
679	

You probably don't need an estimate for a number smaller than 10.
Having rounded the numbers, you should be able to do the simplified sums in your head.

3 Estimate and then calculate the answers to these.

You will probably need to write down the rounded numbers before you calculate your estimate – like you did in question 1.

a)	**Estimate:**	674 – 104 ≈ ___	**Calculation:**	674 – 104 = ___
b)		786 – 453 ≈ ___		786 – 453 = ___
c)		342 + 529 ≈ ___		342 + 529 = ___
d)		111 + 767 ≈ ___		111 + 767 = ___
e)		57 × 4 ≈ ___		57 × 4 = ___
f)		76 ÷ 4 ≈ ___		76 ÷ 4 = ___
g)		699 × 2 ≈ ___		699 × 2 = ___
h)		97 × 3 ≈ ___		97 × 3 = ___

4 These sums have been done on a calculator. First decide if you think they look right, then check with your calculator.

a)	679 + 172 = 7751	Looks correct Yes/No	679 + 172 = ___
b)	867 – 459 = 1326	Looks correct Yes/No	867 – 459 = ___
c)	57 × 3 = 171	Looks correct Yes/No	57 × 3 = ___
d)	990 ÷ 5 = 198	Looks correct Yes/No	990 ÷ 5 = ___
e)	533 + 52 = 585	Looks correct Yes/No	533 + 52 = ___
f)	963 – 159 = 804	Looks correct Yes/No	963 – 159 = ___

Remember to check your answers to see if they seem sensible. If they do not, repeat the calculation carefully.

5 Here is some straightforward practice using your calculator.

a)	154 × 21 = ___	**f)**	1452 + 278 = ___
b)	389 × 11 = ___	**g)**	629 + 290 = ___
c)	645 × 19 = ___	**h)**	2831 + 2389 = ___
d)	176 ÷ 4 = ___	**i)**	372 – 289 = ___
e)	455 ÷ 5 = ___	**j)**	782 – 587 = ___

Test question

Use your calculator to work these out.

What is the product of 135 and 498? ______

What is the sum of 2879 and 1743? ______

What is the difference between 879 and 1265? ______

Divide 465 by 15. ______

Answers and Guidance are given on pp.44-45.

How long did you take?

National Test Questions 3

You should be able to complete these questions in 10–14 minutes.

1 On the grid, draw the reflection of the shape in the mirror line.

You may use a mirror and tracing paper.

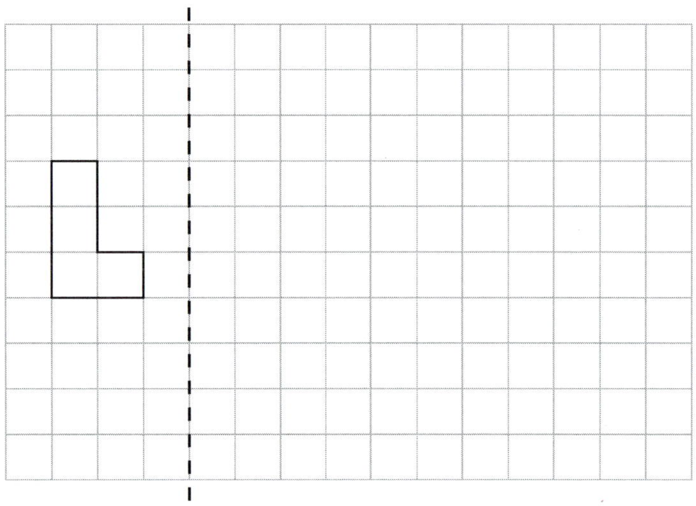

mirror line

1 mark

2 Emma buys these three jars of jam.

What is the total cost of the three jars?

....

1 mark

Show your working. You may get a mark.

Jack buys one jar of cherry jam for 82p.

He pays with a £5 note.

How much change does he get?

....

1 mark

3 Chris did a survey of the number of people who went into shops in one hour.

Number of people who went into a shop

𝍸 stands for 5 people

Shoe shop	𝍸 𝍸 //
Newsagent	////
Post Office	𝍸 𝍸 𝍸 𝍸 //
Bread shop	𝍸 𝍸 ////
Supermarket	𝍸 𝍸 𝍸 //

How many people went into the **Supermarket** in the hour?

....

1 mark

How many **more** people went into the **Post Office** than the **Shoe shop**?

....

1 mark

Here is a part of a bar chart of the information.

Draw in the **missing** bar.

People who went into shops

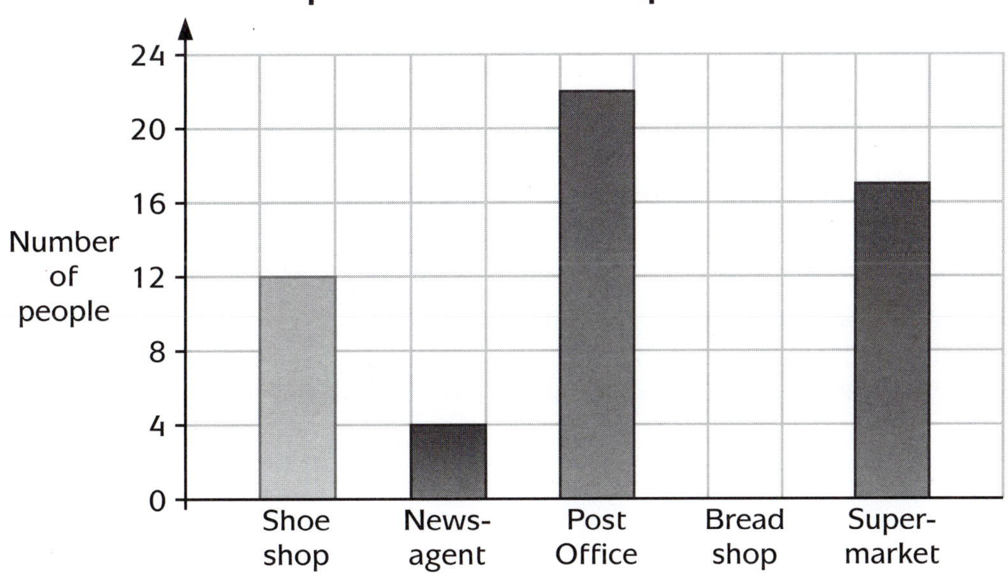

1 mark

4 Here is a row of numbers.

1 2 3 4 5 6 7 8 9 10 11 12 13 14 15 16 17 18

Find three numbers next to each other which add up to 39.
Draw a ring round them.

1 mark

5 Use a calculator to work these out.

$329 \times 67 =$ ☐

1 mark

$216 \div 9 =$ ☐

1 mark

$327 + 876 =$ ☐

1 mark

$984 - 671 =$ ☐

1 mark

6 Here are three badges.

A **B** **C**

You may use a mirror and tracing paper.

Put a tick (✓) in the box if the badge has reflective symmetry.

A ☐ B ☐ C ☐

1 mark

Draw one line of symmetry on this badge.

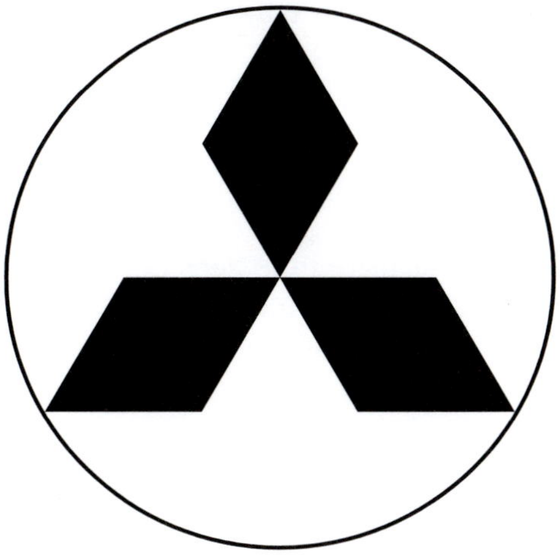

1 mark

7 Here are some apples.

What is the total mass (weight) of these apples?

....

1 mark

8 This calculation has the same number missing from each box.

Write the missing number in the boxes.

$\square \times \square - \square = 42$

1 mark

Answers and Guidance are given on pp.47–48. How long did you take?

Answers and Guidance

1 Number patterns

The work on number sequences in this chapter is towards level 4. More difficult patterns are part of the work of later level 4 and level 5.

1 b) **Add 3 each time.**
c) **Add 9 each time.**
d) **Subtract 4 each time.**
e) **Subtract 7 each time.**

2

a)	1	7	13	**19**	**25**	**31**
b)	24	20	16	**12**	**8**	**4**
c)	15	27	39	**51**	**63**	**75**
d)	33	28	23	**18**	**13**	**8**
e)	1	12	23	**34**	**45**	**56**
f)	100	82	64	**46**	**28**	**10**

If any of your answers were wrong, check that:
- you counted on or back correctly to find the rule
- you followed it accurately.

3 b) 15 19 21 25
add 4 **add 2** **add 4**

c) 29 17 11 8
subtract 12 **subtract 6** **subtract 3**

d) 34 45 56 67
add 11 **add 11** **add 11**

e) 27 42 55 66
add 15 **add 13** **add 11**

If any of your answers were wrong, check by writing the sums you are doing on a spare piece of paper.

4 c) 6 8 12 18 26
add 2 **add 4** **add 6** **add 8**

Rule: **The gap between the numbers increases by 2 each time.**

d) 6 5 8 7 10
subtract 1 **add 3** **subtract 1** **add 3**

Rule: **The gap has a pattern which is 'repeat: subtract 1, add 3'.**

e) 29 24 32 27 35
subtract 5 **add 8** **subtract 5** **add 8**

Rule: **The gap has a pattern which is 'repeat: subtract 5, add 8'.**

These rules are all patterns, look carefully!

5 a) Rule: **The gap between the numbers increases by 1 each time.**

b) Rule: **The gap between the numbers has a pattern which is 'repeat: add 2, subtract 3'.**

c) Rule: **The gap between the numbers has a pattern which is 'repeat: add 5, add 5, add 3, add 3'.**

d) Rule: **The gap between the numbers has a pattern which is 'repeat: add 2, add 3, subtract 1'.**

If you are not sure that your rules are the same as the ones given here, ask an adult to check them with you.

If any of your answers for these rules were wrong, check that:
- you calculated the gaps between numbers correctly
- you wrote down the gaps to make it easier to recognise the rule.

6 a) 44 36 28 **20** **12** **4**
b) 2 13 24 **35** **46** **57**
c) 17 19 24 26 31 **33** 38 40 **45** **47**
d) 20 **24** 28 32 **36** **40** 44
e) 14 **21** 28 35 **42** **49** 56

If any of your answers were wrong, check that:
- you found the correct rules
- you used them to help you work out the sequences.

Test question

4 7 9 12 14 **17** 19 22 **24**

The rule is 'repeat: add 3, add 2'.

Target time for all questions: 30 minutes

Your time for all questions

2 Using timetables

This chapter is working towards level 4. To achieve level 5 you must be able to read and use more difficult tables – see Book 4, Chapter 9 Time.

1 a) **07.41**
b) i) **4 minutes**
ii) **5 minutes**
iii) **12 minutes**
iv) **47 minutes**
v) **1 hour 23 minutes**
c) **3 minutes – Portslade to Hove**
d) **18 minutes – Hove to Haywards Heath**

Answers and Guidance

If any of your answers were wrong, check that:

- you read the correct times off the timetable, e.g. Worthing 07.24; London Victoria 08.47
- you realised that all these problems were subtraction sums in one form or another – if you had difficulty with this, look at 'Solving problems' on pages 26–27
- you worked out the differences between the times correctly, e.g. when working out the total journey time between Worthing and London, you worked out that:
  07.24 to 08.00 = 36 minutes
  08.00 to 08.47 = 47 minutes
  total time = 1 hour 23 minutes
- when working out parts (c) and (d), you calculated the journey times between each pair of stations before answering the question.

2 a) **No, it doesn't arrive until 11 minutes past 8.**
b) **Between Hove and Haywards Heath.**
c) **Between Gatwick Airport and East Croydon.**
d) **08.04**
e) **09.03**

If any of your answers were wrong, check that:

- for parts (b) and (c), you found the times either side of the given time, e.g. in part (b) you found the station that the train was at just before 07.50 – that is 07.41 (Hove) – and just after 07.50, which is 07.59 (Haywards Heath)
- for part (e) you worked out the time difference between 08.11 and 08.27 and then added it to 08.47.

3 a) **The 49 bus arrives first.**
b) **It takes the 20A bus 2 hours 28 minutes to get from Eastham to Southam.**
c) **The 49 bus.**
d) **The 49 bus is leaving Eastable.**

If any of your answers were wrong, check that:

- you looked very carefully at the questions and thought about what you needed to do
- in part (a) you read the times on the timetable and worked out that Bus 20A arrived at 09.30, Bus 49 at 09.02, so the 49 arrived first
- in part (b) you saw that the 20A bus left Eastham at 07.02 and arrived at 09.30 in Southam – you then needed to subtract the times.

Test question

1 Quiz show **2 Sport** **3 12.10 or 00.10**

If any of your answers were wrong, check that:

- you read the table carefully
- you understood that each programme runs until it is time for the next programme to start
- you understood that some questions asked for answers between the programme times
- you managed to add $1\frac{1}{2}$ hours to 10.40 – $1\frac{1}{2}$ hours is 1 hour 30 minutes, which, when added to 10.40 takes you to 12.10 or 00.10.

Target time for all questions: ***25–30 minutes***

Your time for all questions

3 Drawing 2D shapes

You need to be able to draw a range of 2D shapes to be at level 4. At level 5 you have to draw a range of angles accurately and to construct models of 3D shapes – see Book 3, Chapter 4 Nets and Book 4, Chapter 11 Angles.

1 Ask an adult to check the accuracy of your drawing.

The measurement of length and angles must both be correct. If they are not, check that:

- you measured from 0 on your ruler
- you are sure what a right angle looks like
- you can use the protractor to measure angles correctly.

2 a) **50°**
b) **70°**
c) **60°**
d) **30°**

If any of your answers were wrong, check that:

- you put the centre of the protractor on the right place, where the two lines meet
- you used the right scale on the protractor
- you measured the marked angle!

3 Ask an adult to check the accuracy of your drawing.

The measurement of length and angles must both be correct. If they are not, check all the measurements again.

4 **9 cm**

If your answer was wrong, check your measurements.

5 a) **square**

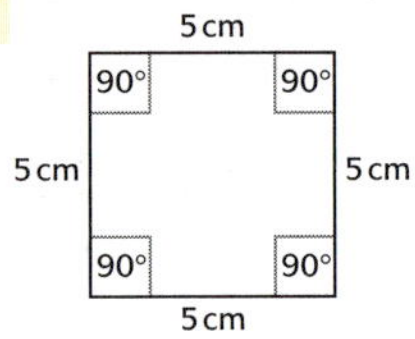

c) **square**

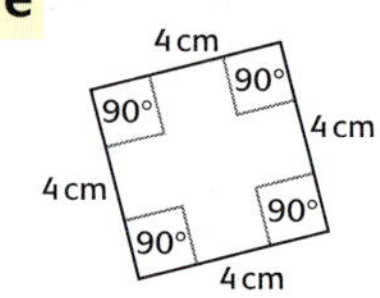

b) **equilateral triangle**

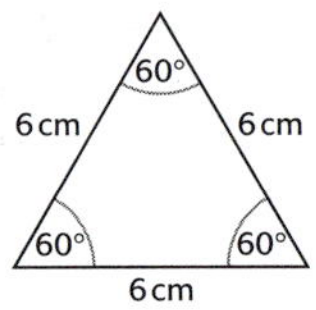

d) **isosceles triangle**

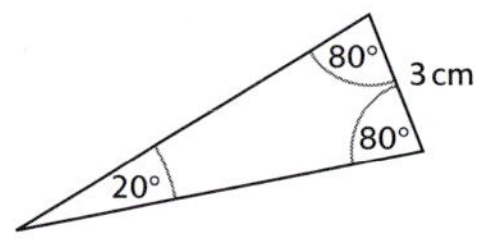

If you did not manage to draw these shapes, check that:

- you measured the angles accurately
- you measured the lengths accurately
- you joined the lines correctly.

Try again but check each step carefully.

Test question

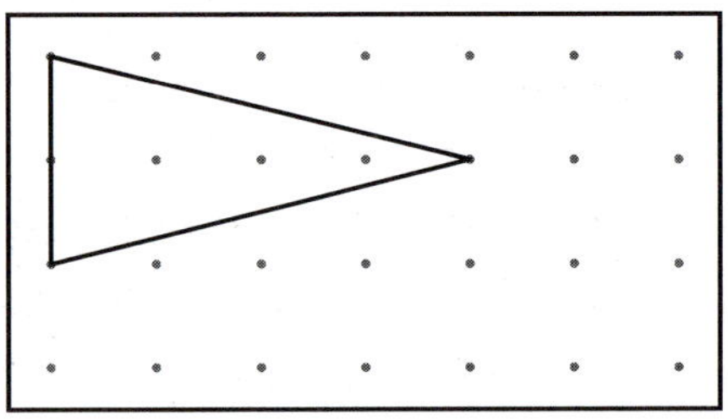

If the shape you drew does not look like this, check that:

- you know what an isosceles triangle is
- you used the dots to help you
- you used your ruler to draw the lines
- you kept your shape within the box.

Target time for all questions: 20–25 minutes

Your time for all questions

4 Missing numbers

This chapter is working towards level 4.

1 a) 6 **–** 4 = 2   2 **+** 4 = 6

b) 9 **–** 2 = 7   7 **+** 2 = 9

c) 4 **+** 9 = 13   13 **–** 9 = 4

d) 24 **–** 14 = 10   10 **+** 14 = 24

The question asks what you notice about each pair of sums. Your answer must show that you understand that:

- when you take away a number from a starting number – and then add it back on again – you end up where you started, and
- when you add a number on to a starting number – and then take it away again – you also end up where you started. Obvious!

2 a) **50** + 5 = 55   g) **110** – 23 = 87

b) **25** – 8 = 17   h) **43** + 56 = 99

c) **19** + 7 = 26   i) **12** + 93 = 105

d) **42** – 13 = 29   j) **419** – 125 = 294

e) **26** + 16 = 42   k) **690** – 123 = 567

f) **79** – 34 = 45   l) **338** + 335 = 673

If any of your answers were wrong, check that:

- you can add and subtract accurately in your head – if you can't there are games in *Collins Success in Maths: Mental Maths* to help you practise
- in the addition sums, you found the missing number *either* by subtracting the number you know from the answer *or* by counting on to the number you know
- in the subtraction sums, you found the missing number by adding the number you know to the answer.

3 a) 29 + **38** = 67   e) 283 + **148** = 431

b) 76 + **5** = 81   f) 543 + **135** = 678

c) 66 + **27** = 93   g) 615 + **414** = 1029

d) 96 + **83** = 179   h) 1542 + **805** = 2347

If any of your answers were wrong, check that:

- you can add and subtract accurately, both in your head and when you write sums down
- if you worked in your head, you used a sensible method, such as adding on hundreds first, then tens and then units – for more help, see *Collins Success in Maths: Mental Maths*.

4 a) 78 – **14** = 64   e) 724 – **372** = 352

b) 92 – **21** = 71   f) 985 – **328** = 657

c) 62 – **19** = 43   g) 980 – **615** = 365

d) 157 – **28** = 129   h) 1198 – **122** = 1076

If any of your answers were wrong, check that:

- you *either* counted on to the answer to find how many had been subtracted, *or*
- you subtracted the answer from the first number in the sum.

Answers and Guidance

5 a) **37** + 46 = 83
b) 21 + **59** = 80
c) 198 – **70** = 128
d) 1348 + **1023** = 2371
e) **2116** – 1138 = 978
f) **711** – 164 = 547
g) 4672 – **2274** = 2398
h) 9856 – **4474** = 5382
i) **21 259** + 51 290 = 72 549
j) 654 + **225** = 879

6 b) 52 + 34 = **86** Check: **86 – 34 = 52** *or* 86 – 52 = 34
c) 82 – 58 = **24** Check: **24 + 58 = 82** *or* 82 – 24 = 58
d) 186 – 145 = **41** Check: **41 + 145 = 186** *or* 186 – 41 = 145
e) 879 – 451 = **428** Check: **428 + 451 = 879** *or* 879 – 428 = 451
f) 587 + 326 = **913** Check: **913 – 326 = 587** *or* 913 – 587 = 326

Don't forget to use what you have practised to check your sums.

Test question

112 + 79 – 191

260 – **134** = 126

Target time for all questions: 30 minutes

Your time for all questions

5 Using multiplication

This page includes work based on knowledge of multiplication at level 3. However, using this knowledge quickly and correctly moves you on to work at level 4. To achieve level 5 you will need to be able to multiply larger numbers – see Book 3, Chapter 3 Multiplying larger numbers.

1 a) 9 × 6 = **54**
8 × 9 = **72**
9 × 9 = **81**
4 × 9 = **36**
3 × 9 = **27**
9 × 5 = **45**

b) 7 × 0 = **0**
10 × 7 = **70**
7 × 5 = **35**
7 × 8 = **56**
9 × 7 = **63**
6 × 7 = **42**

c) 8 × 7 = **56**
9 × 8 = **72**
3 × 8 = **24**
0 × 8 = **0**
8 × 8 = **64**
8 × 4 = **32**

d) 6 × 9 = **54**
6 × 8 = **48**
5 × 6 = **30**
6 × 6 = **36**
3 × 6 = **18**
7 × 6 = **42**

If any of your answers were wrong, check that you really know all your tables, backwards and forwards. You should be able to answer each of these questions instantly!

2 (circled numbers shown in brackets)

35	2	3	4	(5)	6	(7)	8	9	10	11	12
48	(2)	(3)	(4)	5	(6)	7	(8)	9	10	11	(12)
36	(2)	(3)	(4)	5	(6)	7	8	(9)	10	11	(12)
60	(2)	(3)	(4)	(5)	(6)	7	8	9	(10)	11	(12)
28	(2)	3	(4)	5	6	(7)	8	9	10	11	12
54	(2)	(3)	4	5	(6)	7	8	(9)	10	11	12

A factor of a number will divide into that number without a remainder. If you did not find all of the factors for some of these numbers, it is probably because you did not go up the table far enough – e.g. 54 = 27 × 2 and 18 × 3, 48 = 24 × 2 and 16 × 3.

3 (circled numbers in round brackets, boxed numbers in square brackets, crossed-out numbers struck through)

[~~56~~]	45	(30)	[(72)]	(18)	[16]	~~21~~	57	(66)	[80]
39	~~35~~	[(48)]	~~63~~	~~14~~	(~~42~~)	~~28~~	44	~~70~~	[32]
27	(54)	[(24)]	(36)	[40]	(60)	~~49~~	(12)	[64]	50

4 c) **26** e) **23** g) **44** i) **29**
d) **34** f) **15** h) **13** j) **8**

If any of your answers were wrong, check that you understood what you had to do. You were asked to do the sum and then take 1 away from the answer, e.g. 6 × 6 = 36, then 36 – 1 = 35.

If you understood this, then check your multiplication and check your subtraction.

5 (circled numbers shown in brackets)

c)	13	(49)	(35)	29	46	55	(56)
d)	(16)	26	(37)	40	41	(51)	59
e)	(20)	25	(38)	(47)	51	66	79
f)	17	24	(26)	29	(30)	33	(46)

Did you remember that a multiple of a number is one which appears in its table? In parts (d), (e) and (f) you were asked to find numbers which were 2 more than a multiple. Look back at the hint you were given on the left-hand side of the page.

Answers and Guidance

6 a) **Any three of: 18, 27, 36, 45, 54, 63, 72, 81, 90, …**

There are lots more answers. If you have a different answer, ask an adult to check it for you.

b) **Any four of: 1, 2, 4, 5, 8, 10, 20, 40**

c) **8**

d) **6 or 12 or 18 or 24 or 30 or 36 or 42 or 48 or 54 …**

There are lots more answers. If you have a different answer, ask an adult to check it for you.

e) **Any five of: 1, 2, 3, 5, 6, 10, 15, 30**

Test question

2 3 4 5 6 (7) 8 9

Target time for all questions: 25 minutes

Your time for all questions

6 Number lines and scales

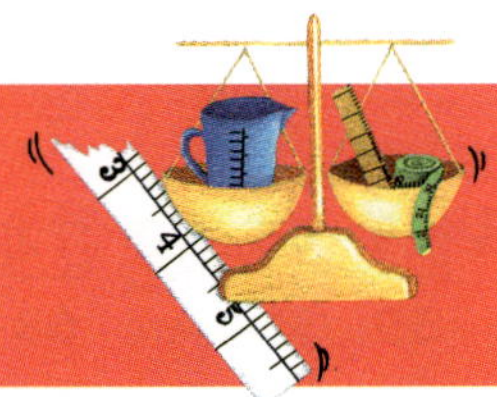

This chapter is working towards level 4. To achieve level 5 you must be able to convert one metric unit to another – see Book 3, Chapter 9 Conversion of units.

1 b)

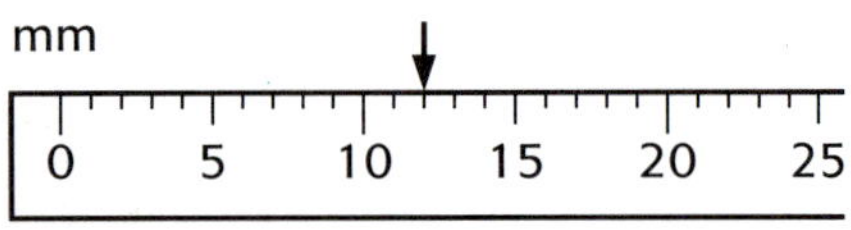

For 12 mm the arrow must be two divisions past 110.

c)

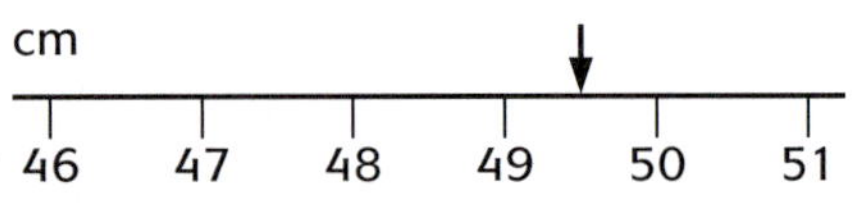

Notice that this number line does not start at zero. $49\frac{1}{2}$ cm is midway between 49 and 50.

d)

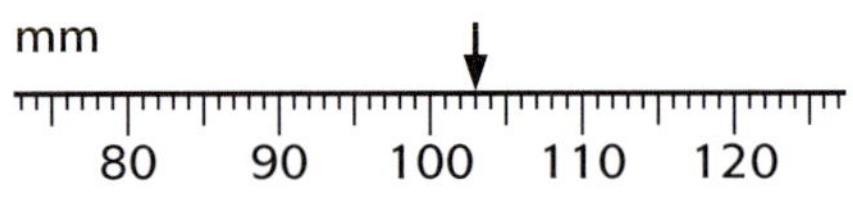

This number line counts in tens. 103 mm is 3 divisions beyond the 100.

You need to be fairly accurate. Use a very sharp pencil and make sure that it is clear where your arrow is pointing.

2 b)

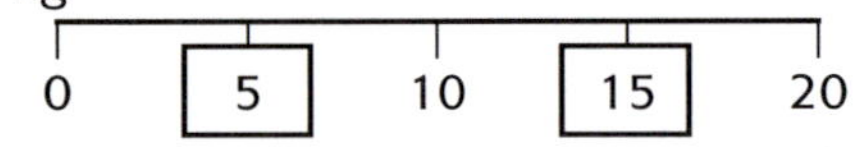

c)

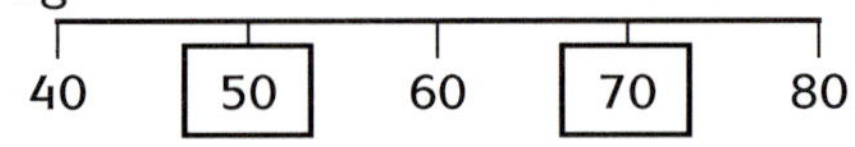

d)

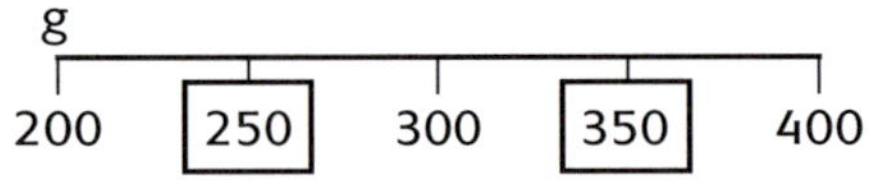

e)

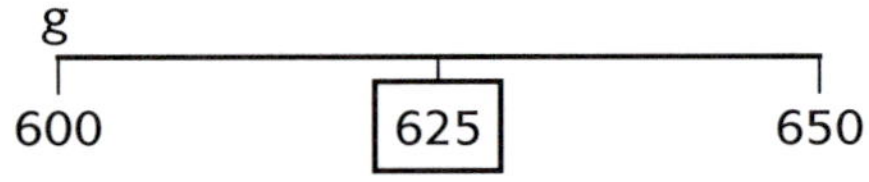

f)

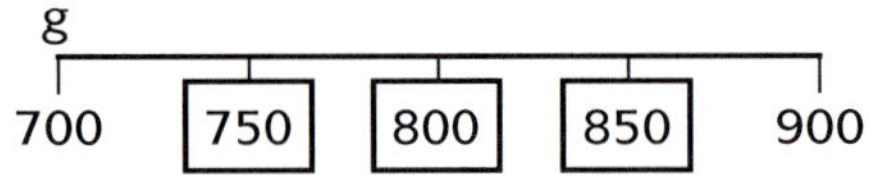

3 a) **530 g** b) **350 g** c) **52 kg** d) **94 kg**

You would get marks if your answers were within these ranges:

a) 525–535 g c) 51–53 kg

b) 340–360 g d) 93–95 kg

If any of your answers were wrong, check that:

- you counted on from the first number on the line
- you worked out what each division was 'worth' correctly
- you can count in 5s, 10s and 50s starting from any number
- you estimated correctly when the arrow was between marks.

4 a)

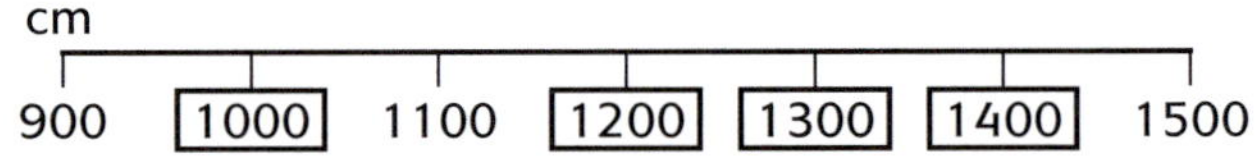

b)

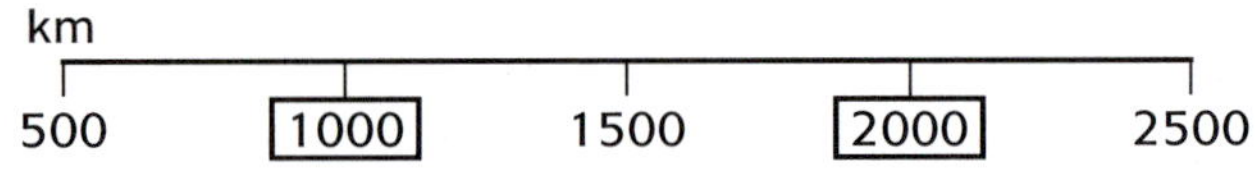

c)

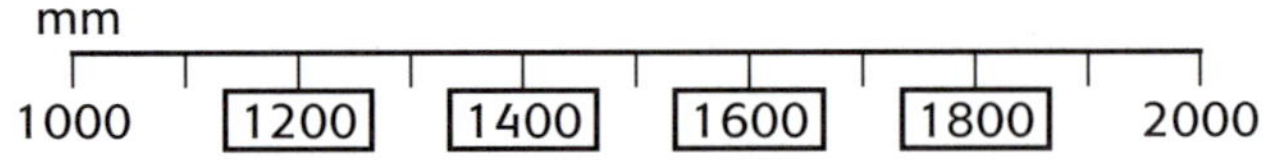

d)

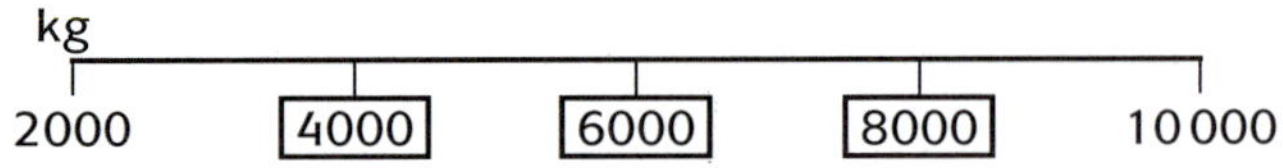

5 a)

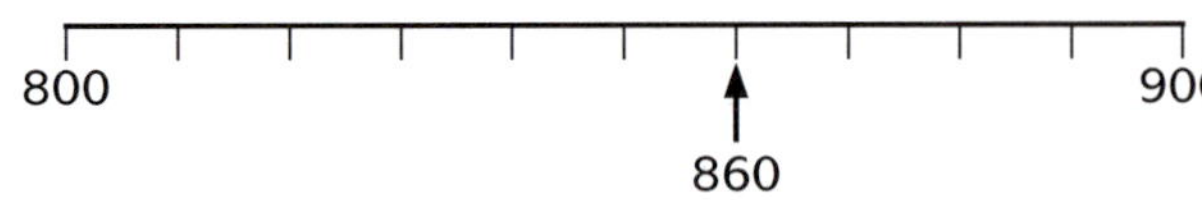

b)

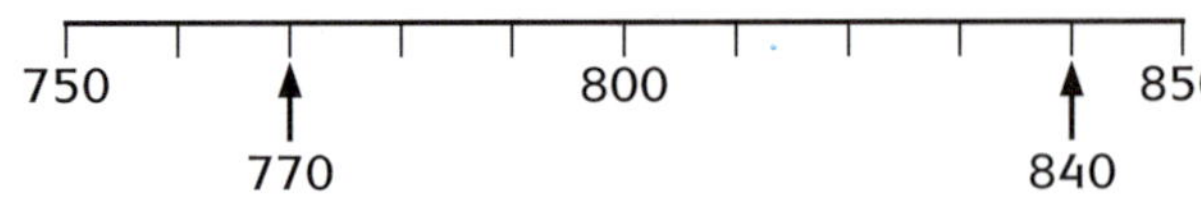

c)

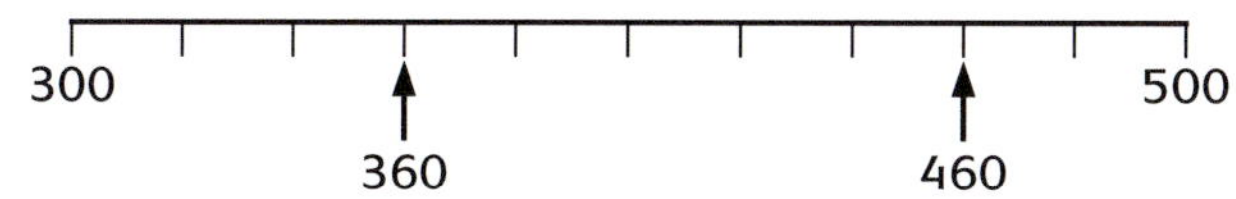

d)

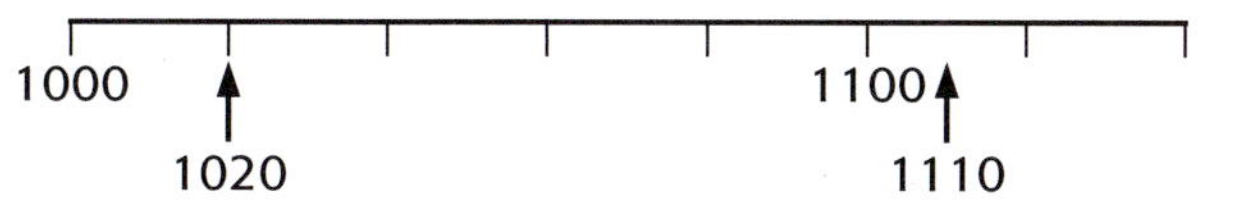

Test question

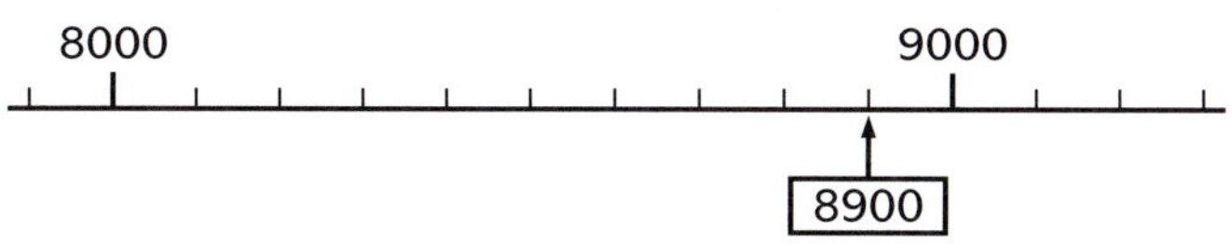

The answer is 8900. If your answer was wrong check that:

- you worked out the divisions correctly
- you counted in hundreds.

Target time for all questions: 15–20 minutes

Your time for all questions

7 Probability

You need to be able to use simple vocabulary associated with probability for level 4. To be working at level 5, you need to be able to express probabilities as fractions, see Book 3, Chapter 2 Probability.

1 a) **True** b) **True** c) **True** d) **B** e) **C**

2 **Likely – because there are more blue marbles than red ones.**

3 In your explanation, you must say that it is likely to be blue because there is only one red marble and there are seven blue marbles. Ask an adult to check your answer.

4 a) **Impossible – there is no 12 on the spinner.**

b) **There is an even chance – there is the same number of odd numbers as even numbers.**

c) **Likely – there are six ways of spinning 8 or less and only two ways of spinning more than 8.**

d) **Unlikely – there is only 1 way of spinning more than 9 and 7 ways of spinning 9 or less.**

e) **Certain – all the numbers are less than 11.**

If any of your answers were wrong, check that:

- you understand what the different words mean
- you counted the numbers correctly.

5 a) **It is impossible to throw a 7 in one throw – there is no 7 on a dice.**

b) **I am certain to throw at least a total of 2 in two throws – I must throw at least 1 each throw, so in two throws I must throw at least 2.**

c) **I am unlikely to throw five 6s in a row – but I just could, so it is not impossible!**

d) **I am likely to score a number less than 5 next throw – there are four ways of throwing less than 5 but only two ways of throwing 5 or more.**

e) **There is an even chance of scoring a 3 or less next throw – there are three ways of throwing a 3 or less (i.e. 1, 2 or 3) and three ways of throwing more than 3 (i.e. 4, 5 or 6).**

Test question

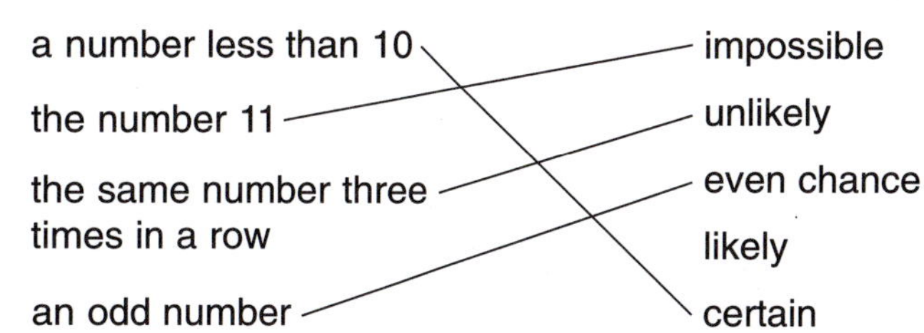

Target time for all questions: 20 minutes

Your time for all questions

8 Perimeters

This chapter includes work at level 4. To reach level 5 you must be able to measure and calculate the perimeters of more complicated shapes – see Book 3, Chapter 8 Area and perimeter and Book 4, Chapter 3 Area and perimeter.

2 a) **6 cm** d) **12 cm**

b) **12 cm** e) **12 cm**

c) **8 cm** f) **10 cm**

If any of your answers were wrong, check that:

- you only counted round the outside of the shape
- you counted each outside edge only once.

If you still find these difficult, try writing the numbers on the diagrams.

3 a) **4 cm** b) **6 cm**

c) There are different ways of putting the squares together, so ask an adult to check your answers.

d) Ask an adult to check the perimeters of your shapes.

If any of your answers were wrong, check that:

- you only counted round the outside of the shape
- you counted each outside edge only once.

4 Ask an adult to check your drawings.

Test question

Shape E has a perimeter of 10 cm.

Target time for all questions: 20 minutes

Your time for all questions

9 Using bar graphs

This chapter includes work leading to level 4. To achieve level 5, you must be able to draw more types of graphs and diagrams and be able to draw more difficult conclusions from the data – see Book 2, Chapter 9 Line graphs and Book 4, Chapter 10 Interpreting data.

1 **Title: The number of different types of vehicle which passed the school in one hour**

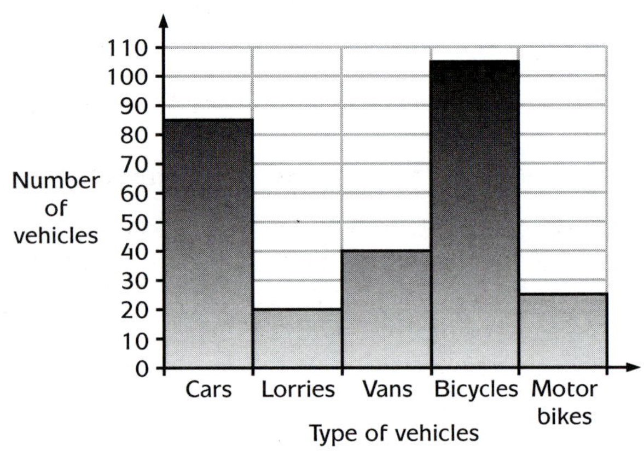

If your graph was wrong, check that:

- you read the numbers in the table correctly
- you counted in tens when you filled in each bar
- you estimated between the lines to show 105 and 25
- your drawing was accurate.

a) **45**

b) **Lorries**

c) **Bicycles and cars**

d) **275 vehicles**

e) **130 two-wheeled vehicles**

If any of your answers were wrong, check that:

- you read from your graph accurately: try again, using a ruler to help you read across the graph accurately
- you can read the scale on the vertical axis – for more help see Chapter 6 Number lines and scales on pages 16–17
- you chose the correct numbers to add or subtract in parts (a), (d) and (e)
- you used the correct mathematics to solve these problems – for more help see Chapter 10 Solving problems on pages 26–7.

2 Title: **A weather graph**

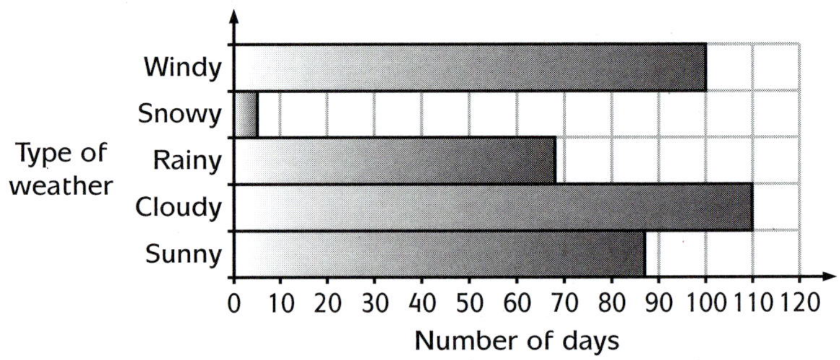

a) **82 more days were sunny than snowy. An answer in the range 80–85 would be acceptable.**

b) **210 days were either cloudy or windy.**

c) **Snowy**

d) **Windy (100 days), cloudy (110 days)**

If any of your answers were wrong, use the same check list as for question 1.

3 Title: **The number of children who stay to dinner on different days of the week**

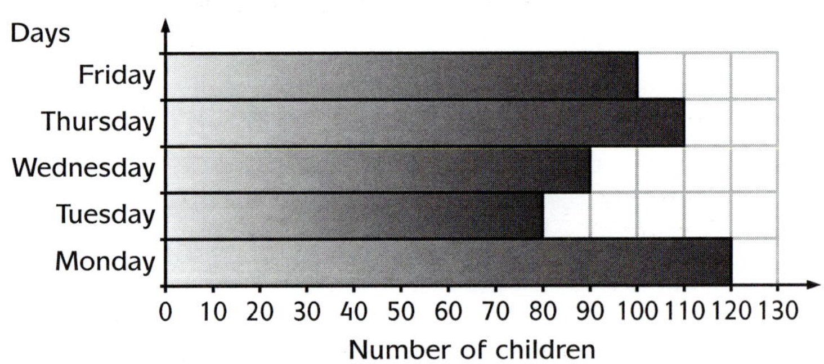

If any of your answers were wrong, use the same check list as for question 1.

Answers and Guidance

Test question

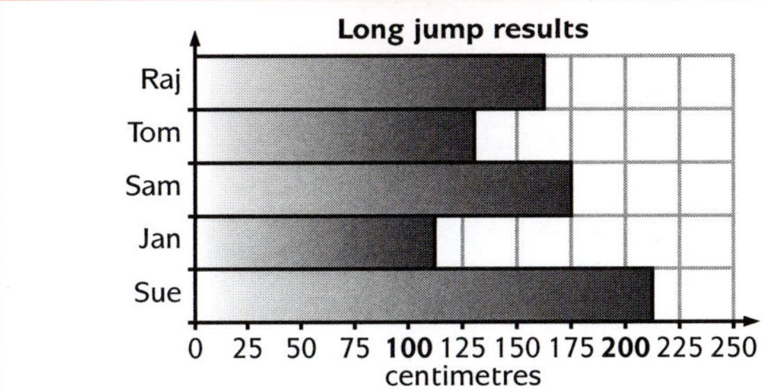

Target time for all questions: 25–30 minutes

Your time for all questions

10 Solving problems

1 a) **24** You had to add 3, 5, 7 and 9.

b) **32** *Either* count on from 46 to 78 *or* subtract 46 from 78.

c) **67** Add 6, 17, 32 and 12.

d) **63** Take 15 away from 78.

e) **20** Multiply 4 by 5.

f) **23** *Either* count on from 56 to 79 *or* subtract 56 from 79.

g) **43** Take 33 away from 76.

h) **Any three of: 4, 8, 12, 16, 20, …**

There are lots more answers. If you have a different answer, ask an adult to check it for you.

2 b) Working: **51 + 13**

Answer: **Annie is 64 years old.**

c) Working: **10 × 9 = 90 and 17 × 10 = 170**
90 + 170 = 260

Answer: **The sum of their ages is 260 years.**

3 a) **£2.80** b) **30p**

If you found this difficult, you could have worked the answers out like this:

a) 2 bags of chips cost 2 × 60p = £1.20
Add this to the cost of the sausage + 50p
and the burger + £1.10
£2.80

Your answer would also be right if you wrote it as 280p or even £2.80p (although you don't usually write the p if you use the £ sign), but not if you wrote £280!

Just leaving a space is dangerous (£2 80). The person marking your answer might not be sure whether you meant £2.80 or £280 so always put in a dot (£2.80) or a dash (£2-80) – it's much safer!

b) Add the price of the cod and the price of the chips.

£1.20 + 60p = £1.80

Look to see if this total is more or less than the cost of fish and chips.

As it is more, take the cost of fish and chips away from this total. £1.80 – £1.50 = 30p

4 a) Working: **99 – 36 = 63**

Answer: **63 grams**

5 **The total cost is £7.20.**

This can be worked out like this:

Cost for 1 child = £3.10 + 50p = £3.60

Cost for 2 children = £3.60 + £3.60 = £7.20

There are other ways of doing this, for instance:

Cost of the coach for 2 children = £3.10 × 2 = £6.20

Cost for the museum for 2 children = 50p × 2
= £1.00

Total cost = £6.20 + £1.00 = £7.20

Test question

The total cost of Jill's order is £4.30.

Ben could buy:

one small mushroom and one medium ham pizza
or
one small tuna and one medium salami pizza.

If any of your answers were wrong, check:

- that you selected the right price from the table – if you found this difficult, look back at Chapter 9 Using bar graphs, pages 24–25
- your arithmetic.

Target time for all questions: 30 minutes

Your time for all questions

Answers and Guidance

11 Reflective symmetry

This chapter includes work at level 4.
To achieve a higher level you need to work with reflections across an axis using co-ordinates – see Book 3, Chapter 10 Reflective symmetry, and Book 4, Chapter 8 Symmetry.

1 When you place the mirror on the line you should see the exact shape shown on the page, reflected in the mirror.

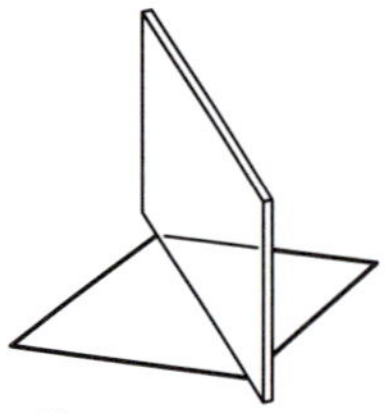

If you did not see this, check that:
- you put the mirror exactly along the line on the drawing
- the mirror was upright on the page.

Try again – this time use other shapes as well.

2 **a) and c) have reflective symmetry.** When a mirror is placed along the mirror line it produces an exact reflection of half of the shape. Shapes (b) and (d) do not have reflective symmetry because there is nowhere that you can put the mirror to give you a reflection that is exactly the same as the shape on the page. These shapes do not have a mirror line.

3 a) 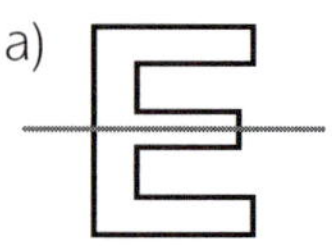 c) 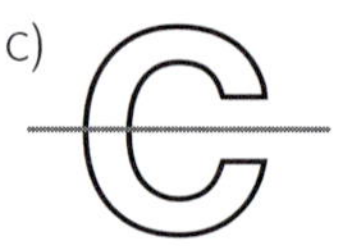 d) 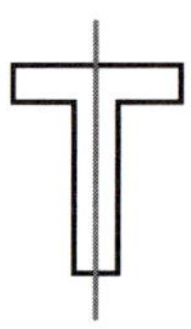

Shape (b) does not have reflective symmetry.

5 You should have marked these shapes.

a) 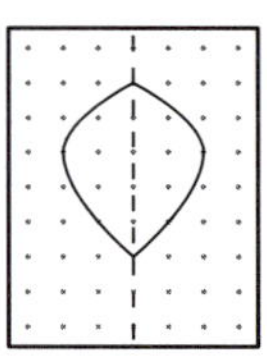 b) 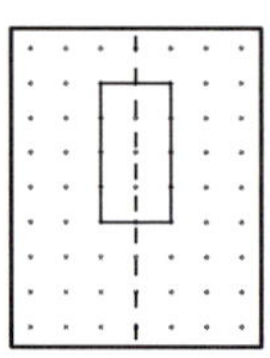 c) 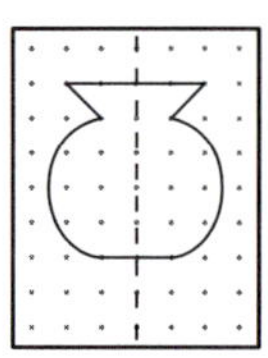

6 You should have marked all these letters, as they each have reflective symmetry as shown below.

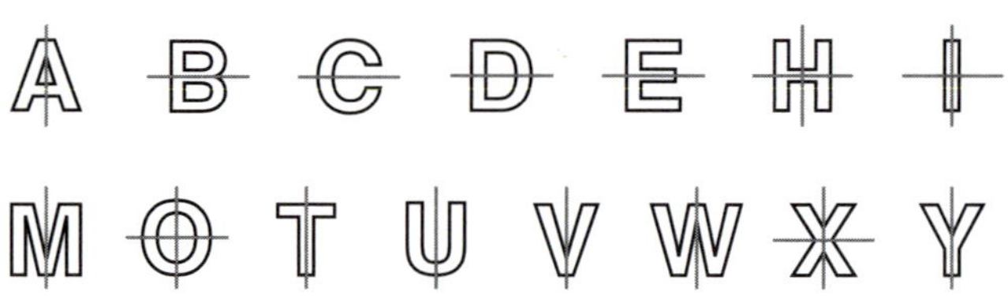

If any of your answers were wrong, check that:
- you tried every letter
- you always drew lines which split the letter into two parts that are reflections of each other.

Test question

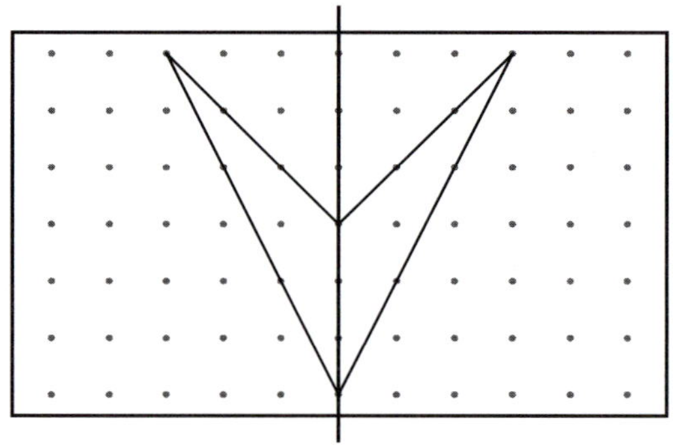

Target time for all questions: 20–25 minutes

Your time for all questions

12 Using a calculator

1 a) 17 + 12 is approximately **20 + 10 = 30**
so 17 + 12 ≈ **30**, actual answer **29**

b) 96 + 31 is approximately **100 + 30 = 130**
so 97 + 31 ≈ **130**, actual answer **127**

c) 68 + 53 is approximately **70 + 50 = 120**
so 68 + 53 ≈ **120**, actual answer **121**

d) 84 + 12 is approximately **80 + 10 = 90**
so 84 + 12 ≈ **90**, actual answer **96**

e) 55 + 34 is approximately **60 + 30 = 90**
so 55 + 34 ≈ **90**, actual answer **89**

f) 21 + 78 is approximately **20 + 80 = 100**
so 21 + 78 ≈ **100**, actual answer **99**

Were your approximations fairly close? If not:
- look again at the guidance in the left-hand column next to the exercise
- make sure you know when to round up to a ten and when to round down.

2

Number	Estimate	Number	Estimate
17	**20**	225	**250**
607	**600**	89	**90**
730	**750**	467	**450**
914	**900**	855	**850**
107	**100**	775	**800**
24	**20**	25	**30**
999	**1000**	679	**700**

If your estimates were not the same as these, again you need to look at the information about when to round to the nearest 10, 50 or 100 given in the left-hand column and practise doing this with other numbers.

Answers and Guidance

3

	Estimate:	Calculation:
a)	650 – 100 = **550**	674 – 104 = **570**
b)	800 – 450 = **350**	786 – 453 = **333**
c)	350 + 500 = **850**	342 + 529 = **871**
d)	100 + 750 = **850**	111 + 767 = **878**
e)	60 × 4 = **240**	57 × 4 = **228**
f)	80 ÷ 4 = **20**	76 ÷ 4 = **19**
g)	700 × 2 = **1400**	699 × 2 = **1398**
h)	100 × 3 = **300**	97 × 3 = **291**

If any of your estimates are very different to the answers here, first check your calculation, then the way you have rounded the numbers in the approximation.

4

a)	679 + 172 = 7751	**No**	679 + 172 = **851**
b)	867 – 459 = 1326	**No**	867 – 459 = **408**
c)	57 × 3 = 171	**Yes**	57 × 3 = **171**
d)	990 ÷ 5 = 198	**Yes**	990 ÷ 5 = **198**
e)	533 + 52 = 585	**Yes**	533 + 52 = **585**
f)	963 – 159 = 804	**Yes**	963 – 159 = **804**

When you check to see if an answer looks right, you should estimate in the way you have been practising.

5
a) 154 × 21 = **3234**
b) 389 × 11 = **4279**
c) 645 × 19 = **12 255**
d) 176 ÷ 4 = **44**
e) 455 ÷ 5 = **91**
f) 1452 + 278 = **1730**
g) 629 + 290 = **919**
h) 2831 + 2389 = **5220**
i) 372 – 289 = **83**
j) 782 – 587 = **195**

Test question

The product of 135 and 498 is 135 × 498 = 67 230.

The sum of 2879 and 1743 is 2879 + 1743 = 4622.

The difference between 879 and 1265 is 1265 – 879 = 386.

465 divided by 15 is 465 ÷ 15 = 31.

*Target time for all questions: **40 minutes***

Your time for all questions

Answers and Guidance

National Test Questions 1

1 **Raj's number is 43.**

If your answer was wrong, check that:
- you read the question carefully
- you understood that the number Raj thought of had 14 subtracted from it.

Try writing the question for yourself like this:

☐ – 14 = 29

CROSS-CHECK **CHAPTER 4** Missing numbers

2 Your answer should look like one of these.

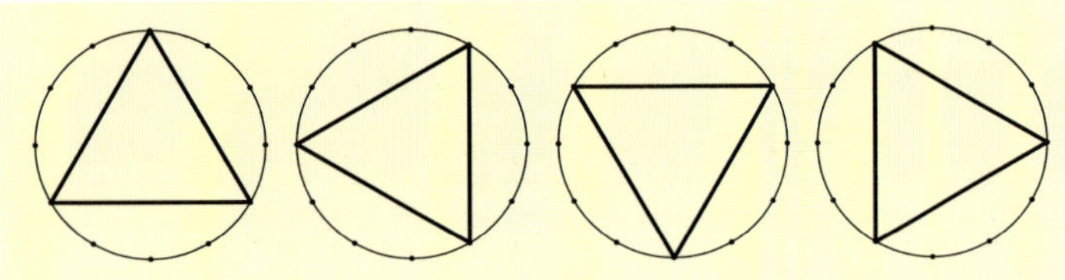

If your answer was wrong, check that:
- you used a ruler
- you drew a three-sided shape, so it had three corners on the circle.

Make sure you drew an equilateral triangle, with all its sides the same length.

You should have used the dots on the circle to help you.

CROSS-CHECK **CHAPTER 3** Drawing 2D shapes

3 6 10 14 11 8 12 16 13 **10** **14**

66 **58** 50 42 **34** 26 18

If any of your answers were wrong, check that:
- you worked out and wrote down the gaps between the numbers you were given
- you looked for a pattern and used it to work out the missing numbers.

CROSS-CHECK **CHAPTER 1** Number patterns

4 a) **7 p.m.**

b) **July and August**

c) **2 hours**

If any of your answers were wrong, check that:
- you used the correct column of opening times – notice that the dates are shown at the top
- you used the correct row of opening times – notice that the times are shown at the side
- you noticed that the right-hand column is for all months except July and August
- you noticed that the top row was the weekday times and that the bottom row was the weekend times.

CROSS-CHECK **CHAPTER 2** Using timetables

National Test Questions 2

1

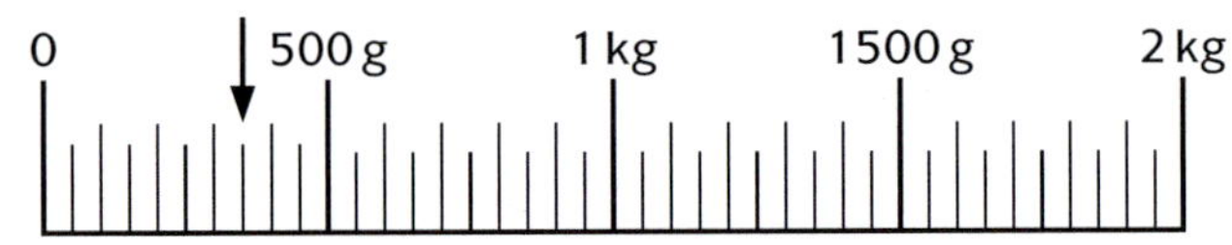

If your answer was wrong, check that you worked out what the divisions on the scale were worth. Look closely at them again and try to work them out.

The section from 0 to 500 has large and small divisions. The large divisions mark every 100 g and the small ones mark every 50 g. So the scale shows 0–50–100–150–200 and so on…

Try again. You can practise by writing in some other weights on the scale and asking an adult to check them for you.

CROSS-CHECK **CHAPTER 6** Number lines and scales

2 Your answer is most likely to look like one of these, but if you did not use complete squares, there are other possibilities. Ask an adult to check.

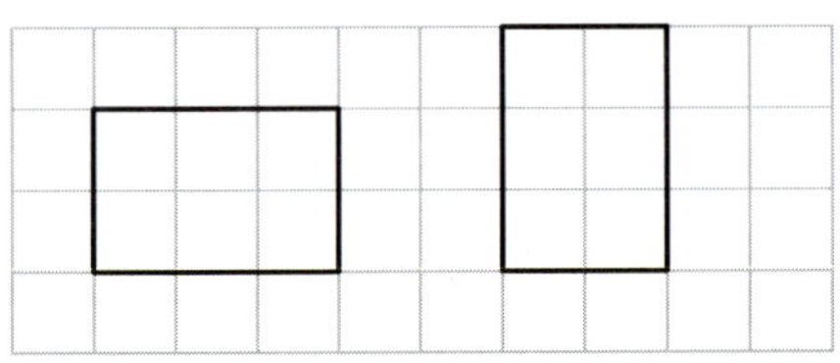

If your answer was wrong, check:
- the perimeter again, you should count 10 outside edges
- that you have drawn a rectangle – make sure you know what one looks like.

A rectangle has two pairs of opposite sides of equal length and a right angle at each corner.

CROSS-CHECK **CHAPTER 8** Perimeters

3 Either **109** or **118** is correct.

If your answer was wrong:
- check that you know your 9 times-table really well
- practise dividing different numbers by 9.

Notice that 99, 108 and 117 are exact multiples of 9 and therefore cannot be the answer.

Work out an answer for every square like this:
97 ÷ 9 = 10 r 7

CROSS-CHECK **CHAPTER 5** Using multiplication

4

a pair of socks with white in them	certain
a pair without white in them	likely
a pair of yellow socks	even chance
a pair of socks	unlikely
a pair with blue in them	impossible

Picking a pair of socks with white in them is likely because all but one pair of socks have white in them.

Picking a pair of socks without white in them is unlikely for the same reason.

Picking a pair of yellow socks is impossible because there aren't any!

Picking a pair of socks is certain; there is nothing else in the drawer.

There is an even chance of picking a pair with blue in them because exactly half the pairs have blue in them.

CROSS-CHECK **CHAPTER 7** Probability

National Test Questions 3

1

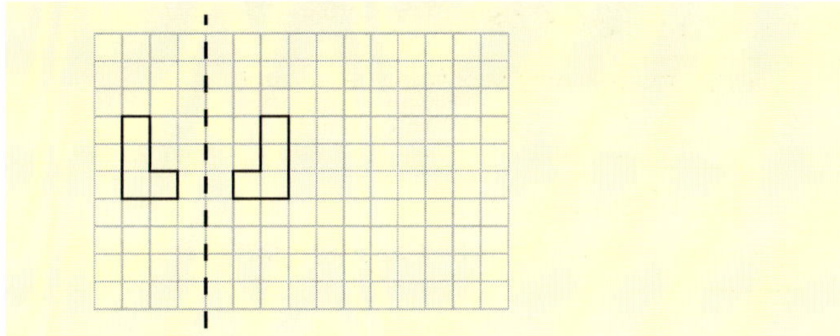

If you did not get this answer, note that:
- the shape was drawn one square away from the mirror line
- you could have used tracing paper
- you could use a mirror to assist you.

CROSS-CHECK **CHAPTER 11** Reflective symmetry

2 a) **£2.17 or 217p** b) **£4.18 or 418p**

This question asks you to add and subtract money. In the first part you need to add the three amounts together.

82p + 70p + 65p = £2.17

The second part asks you to subtract 82p from £5.

You might subtract 82p from £1 and then add on the remaining £4, or you might change the whole £5 into pence and subtract the 82p from 500p.

You need to think carefully about problems, always read the question twice and ask yourself, 'What maths do I need to use?'

CROSS-CHECK **CHAPTER 10** Solving problems

3 a) **17** b) **10**

People who went into shops

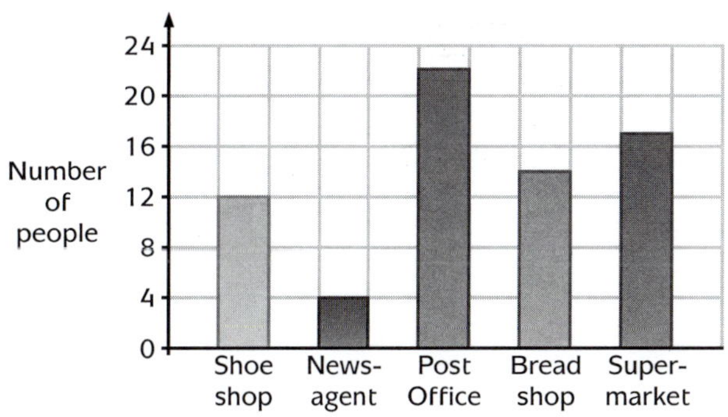

If any of your answers were wrong, check that:
- you counted the tally for each shop correctly – remember 1 𝍸 block represents 5
- you noticed that the scale on the vertical axis went up in fours.

Answers and Guidance

- you realised that 14 people went into the bread shop – you had to work out that the position for 14 on the vertical axis was halfway between the 12 and the 16 and use this information to draw your bar.

CROSS-CHECK **CHAPTER 9** Using bar graphs

4 1 2 3 4 5 6 7 8 9 10 11 **(12 13 14)** 15 16 17 18

If you had difficulty with these answers, notice that:
- the numbers had to add up to 39 and be next to each other
- you probably had to try out different numbers which are next to each other to find ones which add up to 39

and check that:
- you did not make mistakes with your addition.

CROSS-CHECK **CHAPTER 10** Solving problems

5 329 × 67 = **22 043**

216 ÷ 9 = **24**

327 + 876 = **1203**

984 – 671 = **313**

If any of your answers were wrong, you need to check that you are sure how to use your calculator. Ask an adult to help.

Did you remember to work out if your answers were sensible and repeat the calculation if they were not?

CROSS-CHECK **CHAPTER 12** Using a calculator

6 A ✓

B ☐

C ✓

You should have drawn one of these lines of symmetry.

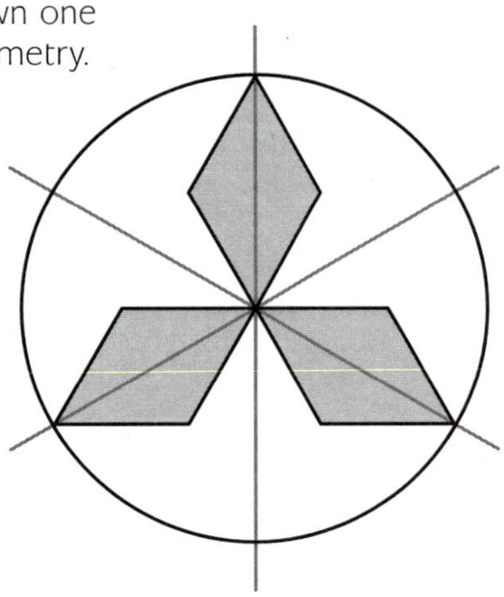

If you did not draw a correct line of symmetry, did you remember about the mirror line? Try again, using either tracing paper or a mirror.

7 **1700 g**

If your answer was wrong, check that:
- you worked out the value of each division on the scale correctly
- you noticed that each small division stands for 50 g
- you counted in either 50 s or 100 s

If you did this, did you count correctly?

CROSS-CHECK **CHAPTER 6** Number lines and scales

8 **7 × 7 – 7 = 42**

To get the answer right you must have the same number in each box.

If you know your 7 times-table well, you will have seen that 42 was a multiple of 7 and that 7 was a good number to try out first (you might have tried 6 on the same basis).

If you did not see this, it would be sensible to have tried any number. Then you could have tried a bigger or smaller number, depending on what you found out. This method of working is called 'trial and improvement'.

CROSS-CHECK **CHAPTERS 5** Using multiplication and **10** Solving problems

MODULE 2 | **Homelink Book A** | New Cambridge MATHEMATICS

Name .... **Class** ....

These activities support the work your child is doing in mathematics at school. Please help your child with them.

- ■ It is best not to take your child away from another enjoyable activity to do them.
- ▲ Encourage your child to see that there are often lots of different ways to do something, and there is very often more than one 'right' answer.
- ● Most of all, make it fun!

How to use this book

The activity to do is dated to show when it will be talked about in class. Please send the book back by then. You can record anything you think the teacher might like to know, or that you would like to remember in the space at the bottom of the page. Your child could draw a face, smiling or sad, in that space to show how they enjoyed the activity.

The borders are designed as starting points for conversation; you could play guessing games, counting games, or colouring games. Whatever you do, have fun!

The cover game boards can be used for several different games. Play one whenever you have some quiet time together. Let your child colour the pictures.

Cover games

You need: 2 players, two sets of 1–9 number cards you have made from a cereal box to fit the spaces on the back cover, two 1–6 dice and counters or buttons.

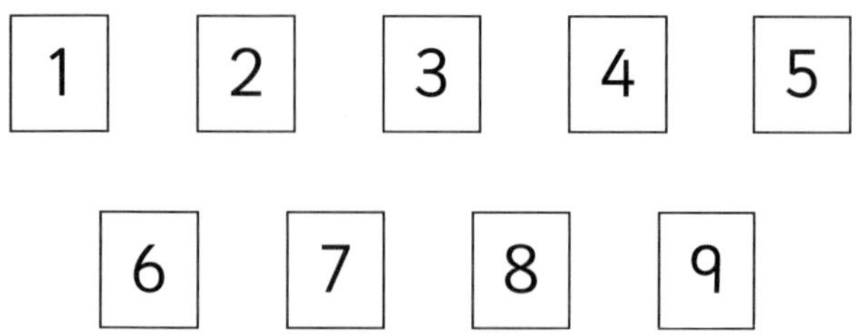

Learning objectives: the game on the back will help your child to see that some numbers are of higher value than others, to think about a strategy for winning and to do mental addition. The game on the front will give them more experience with adding numbers mentally.

Game 1 *(back cover)*

Shuffle the cards and place them face down on the table. One player is Rapunzel and one is the witch.

Take turns to take a card and work out where to place it. The object is to place four cards on your tower so that the larger numbers are at the top of the tower, and the lower numbers are lower down the tower. So if you pick up a 9, you will want to place it in your top space. If you pick up 1 it will go in the bottom space. The problem comes with what you do with 5 or 6! You just have to take a chance. If you pick up a card you already have, put it back at the bottom of the pile and take a new card.

Once a card is placed, it cannot be moved so if you put 8 in your top space and then pick up a 9, you must keep that 9 in front of you. You cannot place a high number below a lower one.

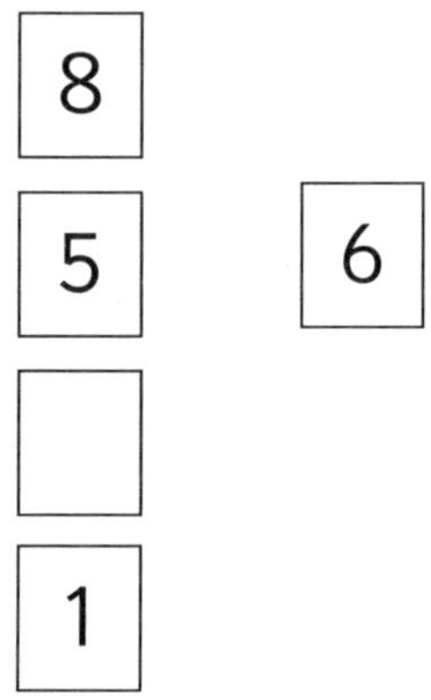

6 cannot be placed because it cannot go below 5.

When both players have picked up 4 cards each they add up the numbers on the cards left in front of them. The winner is the player with the lowest total.

So if one player has a 1 and a 9 left their score is 10 and if the other player has just a 6 left, the player with just 6 left wins.

Every time your child wins a game they can colour in one of the pictures at the side of the game.

Game 2 *(front cover)*

If you don't have two 1–6 dice use two sets of 1–6 cards shuffled together. One player is Rapunzel and one is the witch.

Take turns to throw the dice (or take two cards). Add the scores and cover the number on your person. If that number is already covered, you can't cover a number that turn.

The winner is the first player to cover all the numbers on their person.